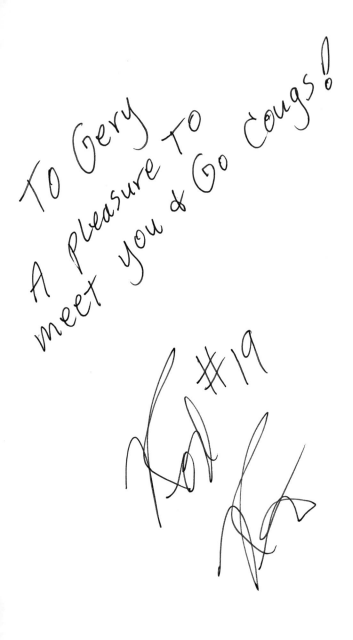

To Gery
A pleasure To
meet you & Go cougs!

#19

PRAISE FOR

One of my most gratifying coaching experiences: to watch Rod Retherford fight such formidable, personal adversity, and somehow still succeed at the demanding level of PAC-10 football while conquering his personal demons.

> — **Jim Walden**, Head Coach Washington State University, 1977-86. Coached eight seasons at Iowa State University and when a player was one of 33 selected by the Denver Broncos in the first AFL Draft in 1960.

This story is excellent for anyone called too small, too fat, too tall, too slow, etc. The answer remains the same; set your eyes on your goal and never give up! Life is a 'Test of will'.

> — **Bobby Bowden,** Head Coach, Florida State University, (tied with Penn State's Joe Paterno as the all-time winningest Division 1-coach in total victories).

Rod Retherford's story is a moving chronicle of one undersized man's great desire to achieve and to compete. His efforts in the rodeo, major college football and overcoming a tragic accident are inspirational and make for very interesting reading.

—**Tom Osborne,** Athletic Director and former head football coach for 25 years at the University of Nebraska. Served six years in Congress representing Nebraska's 3rd Congressional District.

The true emotion of this story will run you from one end of the field of life to the other. An inspiring story of tenacity in the face of adversity.

—**Don James,** Head Football Coach University of Washington 1975-1992, Member College Football Hall Of Fame. As a quarterback for the University of Miami he set five school passing records.

This is a wonderful, good-feeling story of a small, in physical size, young man, but obviously a giant in determination, courage and desire.

—**Steve Spurrier,** Head Football Coach, the University of South Carolina. He was a two-time All-American and is a member of the College Football Hall of Fame as a player. He won the Heisman Trophy in 1966. He coached the University of Florida football team to six SEC championships and one National Championship in 1996.

An affirmation and testimony that anyone can accomplish great things one step, one play, one game, and one day at a time.

—**Pete Brock,** Offensive lineman, University of Colorado, All-American, Hula Bowl All-Star, Chicago Tribune All-Star, Colorado's Team of the Century. NFL New England Patriots—'76-88' both a center and a guard, and ten years as a starter. 1979 Unsung Hero Award; 1984 Jim Lee Hunt Award; 1985 Ed Block Memorial Courage Award (NFL); 1986 Miller Lite NFL Lineman of the Year. Patriots Football Weekly selected Pete for their Patriots Team of the Century at his center position.

Rod Retherford is a shining example of all that is right in sports. Perseverance, toughness, and an amazing will to succeed are all over his amazing story. ROD makes me proud to be a fellow Coug.

—**Drew Bledsoe,** WSU Quarterback 90-92, All-American, PAC-10 Conference Player of the Year as a junior, # 1 overall draft pick 1993 NFL, starting QB for the New England Patriots, and during the 1994 season set single game record in pass completions (45) for the Patriots, led the NFL in passing yards (4555), and became the second NFL quarterback to ever complete 400 or more passes in a season. Super Bowl Championship (2001, Patriots), and Bledsoe currently owns the Patriots' franchise career passing records for attempts, completions, yards, and touchdowns.

There is a story about an old mule who fell down the well. The farmer decided he was not worth the trouble so he decided to bury him with sand. But as he poured it down the shaft the mule kept shaking it off until it had filled the well and the mule simply walked off the top. The story of ROD is just such an example of persistence, determination, and patience revealing how one man can turn his stumbling blocks into stepping stones. He is an example to all of us how, in this vale of tears, it is preferable to view the glass half-full so that we can overcome the majority who grovel in half-empty.

—**Todd Christensen,** five-time All-Pro tight end 1983-1987 caught 349 passes 1983-1986, then an NFL record. Twice he led the NFL in receptions. He played on two Super Bowl champion teams —the 1980 Oakland Raiders and the 1983 Los Angeles Raiders.

Dogged determination, pride, passion and perseverance only begin to define ROD. This inspirational story will have a lasting impact on every reader.

—**Bill Rasmussen,** Founder, ESPN, Entrepreneur, noted by journalists in 1994 as ". . . one of 40 individuals who had the greatest impact on the world of sports over the previous 40 years."

ROD is for kids everywhere, the ones being told that they can't do it, they're too short, too small—this story will tell them to believe in themselves because they can make their dreams happen. And for the adults who control the opportunities—this says loud and clear, let those kids reach for the brass ring.

—**Mark Rypien,** WSU Quarterback 1984 and 1985, the WSU number two all time passing and total offense leader. All-American 1984, 1985 and was named top quarterback in the Pac-10 Conference in 1985. MVP Super Bowl XXVI, Washington Redskins. In his 11 NFL seasons, Rypien completed 1,466 of 2,613 passes for 18,473 yards and 115 touchdowns. He also rushed 127 times for 166 yards and 8 touchdowns. He is one of five players to throw for at least 300 yards in his first NFL game.

Inspiration can come from a wide variety of sources as we move through life, but no source is more meaningful than inspiration generated from a real life story. Rod's story will inspire all readers, as it did me.

—**Dick Vermeil,** UCLA head coach 1974-75, led the Bruins to their first conference championship in 10 years, and a win in the Rose Bowl over an undefeated and number 1 ranked Ohio State. NFL Coach, Kansas City, St. Louis (Super Bowl XXXIV Championship), and Philadelphia. Vermeil was named "Coach of the Year" on four levels: High School, Junior College, NCAA Division I, and the NFL.

The reading was very inspirational to all those who strive to achieve a purpose in life. His accomplishment may not be the pinnacle of what the world views as success, but Rod did the maximum with what God gave him, and he achieved his ultimate goal.

—**Jerome Kersey,** Longwood College, Virginia. Virginia State Hall of Fame. NBA: Portland, LA Lakers, Milwaukee, San Antonio (world championship team). 1987, Second behind Michael Jordan in the NBA Slam-Dunk Competition. 1987–88 he averaged 19.2 points and 8.3 rebounds, was part of the nucleus of a strong Portland team that made it to the NBA Finals two out of the next three years (1990 and 1992).

Tremendous story of a young man whose determination you'll end up admiring as much as any athlete you've ever known—it will be an inspiring story for everyone who reads it.

—**Lee Corso,** analyst and commentator for ESPN

Rod Retherford has a life story that definitely should be preserved in print. He is a shining example of what can be accomplished through the on-going gift of positive attitude and the strong will to never give up. The book ROD gives us a definitive role-model who has experienced and overcome tremendous adversity.

—**Bill Pearl,** Former Mr. America, Mr. USA, and five-time Mr. Universe

ROD

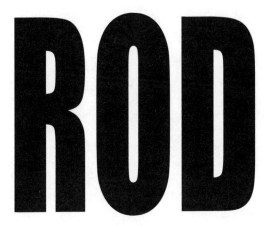

JOHN A. KURI

SEVEN LOCKS PRESS

SANTA ANA, CALIFORNIA

Seven Locks Press
P.O. Box 25689
Santa Ana, CA 92799
(800) 354-5348

Individual sales: This book is available through most bookstores or can be ordered directly from Seven Locks Press at the address above.

Quantity Sales: Special discounts are available on quantity purchases by corporations, associations and others. For details, contact the "Special Sales Department" at the publisher's address above.

Cover Design by John Kuri
Interior Design by Kira Fulks • www.kirafulks.com

Printed in the United States of America

Library of Congress Cataloging-in-Publication Data is available from the publisher

ISBN: 978-0-9801270-7-2
0-9801270-7-6

DEDICATION

For the ones who have been stopped from achieving
their dreams because someone has told them
over and over again, "You are too small."

Rod at Washington State University, 1981

Acknowledgement

Thank you to the many friends and family who offered us their recollections of Rod's life. They include Dennis and Sherry Adkins, Steve Baack, L.J. "Pete" Baucum, Richard Boyer, Calvin Clark, Rod Commons, Jan Arnold Crawford, Jessie Elliott, Gary Farnsworth, David Gibbs, Marvin Gibbs, Gary Gregg, Mitch Gregg, Bill Gribble, Max Hull, Don Jones, Brad Krayer, Ron Kulm, Kelly Lemons, David Liberty, Brent Maddox, Larry Mathews, Rob McClain, Andy Mosby, Mike Peterson, J.R. Smith, Chuck Toste, Joe Sturza, Junior Tupuola, Mike Walker, Harold Wheeler, Gene Winett, Ken Woody, and especially Uncle Vic Retherford, Jim and Betty Retherford, Chris Retherford, Stacey Snow Retherford, and Rick's spirit who visited me a lot.

A very special thank you to Coach Jim Walden, also to the following for their contributions: Rock Caley, The Coug Gals: Karyn Gorman—Jill Gorman—Paige (Gorman) Williams—Kasey Gorman, Darrell Ceciliani, Garth Dano, Steven Grant, Barbara Lynn Kowaleski, Donald Kramer & Lori Van Zee, Feturah G. Miller, Darl Roberts & Kenny Eng, Paul Sumner, Corwin Stephan, George Werner, Brian Wolfe, and especially to the man who inspired this literary endeavor, Doug Gorman.

FOREWORD

This is a book about GRIT...the kind that makes a person dare to reach higher than anyone thought possible.

This is the story of a "little bitty" fellow who has never learned to spell the words "can't" and "quit"...and probably never will.

Why would he...after where he has been and the life experiences he has had!

Sick and tired of people telling him he was too small to do a lot of athletic activities, he pushed the bar aside and kept on reaching.

The coaches must have been afraid for his life when he would hurl his eighty-pound body into the fray called football.

But at age 13, standing four feet-ten inches...he jumped on the back of a rodeo bull and rode him and he tasted success. Oh it was the sweet taste he had been hungering for, and he set out to find some more.

And he surely did despite traveling down a road with a lot of bumps.

He found his greatest success as a Washington State University Cougar varsity football player.

I am a Cougar, an old one. It was Washington State COLLEGE when I landed there after four years in the US Marines in 1950. I grew up in the Corps, so I had some understanding of perseverance. And when I heard the story of Rod Retherford.

I wanted to help lead as many people as possible to the story of this remarkable competitor.

John Kuri is the author. His pace is swift and the story is thrilling. I'm sure you will enjoy his work.

In fifty-four years of broadcasting all manner of college football and every other sport known, one learns to see the competitor, he or she will stand out given a chance...and it is these who inspire...who light the candle in others.

Good Luck Rod Retherford!

Keith Jackson
WSU-Class of '54

PROLOGUE

He had survived all the wounds life could throw at a young man, or so he thought. His ample experience had taught him the body heals a lot faster than does the mind—and this fact was about to play out in spades.

Rod Retherford had made it through the first twenty-one years. He had outlived all of the bullshit that God's green earth could seem to throw at him, that stuff of the teen years that can shape destiny. He had made it out of John Day, leaving behind his eastern Oregon hometown of twelve hundred hard working souls. Ambition and passion propelled him past four years recently lost to drugs and booze, those tools often used to blast pain from our waking thoughts. Rod's life was vaporizing with each beer, whiskey, and joint since that June day of 1974 when he witnessed his big brother, James "Rick" Retherford, his closest friend in all things, die at seventeen tender years in a freak accident of the rodeo.

It was not enough to suffer the early and senseless loss of a loved one, the event lived on with the survivors. That was a cruel truth about life that must be learned—nature's wicked way of building character. For the young it was one giant step across a chasm that only experience can prepare them for. In this case it would rip the fiber of the Retherford family, turning them from quiet hardworking God-fearing folks, reducing the sons from students, athletes, and fun loving pranksters, to victims of self-doubt, blame, and remorse. Not Jim, Betty, or Rod's younger brother Chris, were spared consequences. The family and their home, a gathering place for friends of the boys, was now a fractured shell of an earlier and innocent day.

But on this September day of 1980, sitting in the front seat of his electric blue Dodge Colt with its bright white interior, Rod was fixed on the site of his blood-soaked and motionless arms.

"Wow! This was a short life," he uttered. He was in the center of a vortex of panic where no one would have heard those profound words coming from a man who in a heartbeat before had become a quadriplegic in yet another accident. But like the eye of the hurricane, there was a calmness that took over amidst the trauma. Rod had managed to tune out the collective hysteria swirling around the car.

Twenty-five minutes earlier his heart was pumping, propelling him through his first morning of man-to-man drills since Washington State University Cougar head coach Jim Walden had said two magic words: "Full Ride." A lot of miles down life's pot-holed road had lead Rod to those words. This cowboy had been a walk-on to WSU's football program months earlier and earned his place amongst the veterans and the boys with the scholarships that came from far away places like Southern California's Compton. Not too bad for a kid who was five feet four inches when he graduated from high school.

Coach Walden's friendly smile and southern accent would have put anyone at ease, but Rod had walked into this office with the weight of a lifetime of circumstance crushing that ambition and passion of his. He looked at the man behind the desk and said with that deliberate style and southern sounding voice, "Coach, I love this program—and I wanna play for you. But I can't make enough money to afford tuition and stay alive. My folks don't have any money. I'm working two jobs, mucking out horse stalls, doing the studies, but I don't know how to make this work. I got no problem working, there just isn't enough time."

Rod barely knew Walden. Yes, they had been on the same training turf for months, but most of Rod's dialog was with the defensive back coaches, men like Harold Wheeler. And, when in the trenches one does not climb out to speak with General Tommy Ray Franks just because he is standing there. You take up whatever it is with your Lieutenant. But this was something that Rod knew had to be said to the man himself.

Rod had earned Coach Wheeler's respect from early on. Right after walking-on Rod knew he must do something to be noticed, and Tom Ramburg became the target of that determination during a scrimmage. Playing free safety Rod read a play put in motion by the scout team at the exact moment the quarterback pitched the ball to Ramburg. As Tom came around the corner into the clear Rod, forty-five pounds lighter, nailed him head on. That was it. As Ramburg's heels went into the air Rod had proved he was worthy of the training he was hoping to receive and the jersey he was to wear. When Rod got up hearing the guys on the sideline whooping and hollering at that great defensive hit, he saw Wheeler wearing a big smile, and then came the coach's nod of recognition. "Guess that worked," Rod thought.

Tom Ramburg was picking himself up as Rod heard a familiar voice say, "Crazy man. You're the Kamikazee kid." Mike Walker, a teammate and friend who had encouraged Rod to walk-on to WSU, was grinning as he jogged past Rod. Mike knew Rod was fearless from their junior college days. He had told Rod "If you're a hitter, you'll make the team."

Rod had been riding twenty-four hundred pound bulls since he was thirteen. He said to Walker, "I'm a bull rider. I ain't duckin' my head for no one."

When Rod was a high school sophomore he had wanted to scream those words to his school's football coach.

"You're too short! Don't waste my time. I don't care how hard you work. I'll never play you, not for one second. You wanna be a helper, carry towels, fine." So said John Day Oregon's Grant Union High School varsity football coach to sophomore Rod Retherford.

"What an asshole," Rod had thought. All five feet and ninety-three pounds of him looked on at the athletic authority, the guy with the key to this teen's dreams, and wanted to say, "I'm a bull rider. Do you really think I'm gonna worry about some one hundred eighty-five pound running back? I've been busting broncs since I was thirteen."

Instead, young Rod sucked it up and went on. At home he lied to his dad, Jim, when he said, "I don't feel like playing football this year." If he had told the truth he knew that Jim would have cussed out the varsity coach and probably have started a fight with him. No one was going to deny one of Jim Retherford's boys. That attitude, while appreciated later, was a source of painful embarrassment during the school years.

Growing up a Retherford had meant hard work. Jim treated his three boys the same way, each as his own person, each without regard to size. This made Rod tough because his sibling's physical development was on par with their ages and year in school while Rod was behind the growth curve and had been pushed one year ahead in school. He was always the smallest in his class. As youngsters all three boys did a lot of pushups, sit-ups, and would lie on their backs while a brother would jump up and down on the stomach of the one lying down to further develop their abdominal muscles.

Having come through so much to end up in front of Coach Jim Walden, the man in charge of Washington State University's football future, the guy who was developing one the best PAC 10 defensive squads, and say "I can't stay with the program," was unthinkable. But Rod had reached this conclusion, and Harold Wheeler knew this was a conversation for Coach Walden.

Jim looked up at Rod, that big grin across his strong jaw. "Where you from, boy?"

"John Day, Oregon, coach."

Jim started laughing. "Heck, I thought you'd say the south. In fact, I really thought you were going to say Alabama."

"Funny. I was thinking about walking-on to Alabama when Mike Walker told me about WSU."

Jim looked at him for a moment, then smiled. "You can stop worrying about money, Rod. Today we decided to give full-ride scholarships to three walk-ons and you're one of them. Congratulations."

"Full-ride!" The gates had opened. Rod Retherford, the kid that was too short, who grew up in a small town, and like many might have spent his life within its confines never believing in the dream, had stepped into the future with those two words. He was playing in the PAC 10. He could not even allow his mind to accept that this was a road to the NFL.

As a kid, sitting in front of the family's ten inch black and white television he had watched PAC 10 powerhouses like USC and UCLA playing Notre Dame, Ohio State, and Michigan. Rod Retherford was going to play in games against the giants he had grown up watching. This was the big time.

His other choice in life might have been continuing work with his dad hauling trash in John Day. This was something he had more time into then he ever wanted, but it had to be done in those years after Rick's death, when Jim's life turned into a hell on earth. But life had taken Rod away from John Day, to one of the great universities of the Pacific Northwest. He knew it was hard work that had unlocked the door.

But a single shot from a revolver had just rendered everything that Rod had learned almost meaningless. He didn't know it, but the bullet was resting between vertebrae in his neck.

Rod looked up from his lifeless arms and hands and over his right shoulder to see that blood was pumping out of his neck, pumping the life out of his body. The stream of crimson had soaked Junior Tupuola who had been riding in that white back seat. Junior was freaking out, not knowing what to do for his friend and teammate.

But Rod knew it was a matter of seconds before his body would be lifeless. That pumping blood streaming across the back of the car had to be stopped. In the calmness that had overcome him he said very firmly, "Junior, you have to listen to me. You have to put pressure on my neck and stop the bleeding. As hard as you can, you have to stop the bleeding."

Junior was Samoan. He was a big boy. He was strong. If anyone would have the strength to do this it was Junior. The other teammate in the car, Samoa Samoa, could have too, but he had run for help trying to get an ambulance. Junior had to act without hesitation.

Junior ripped his shirt off and stuffed it against the right side of Rod's neck. He needed to get a grip on Rod but the small car was no match for Junior's size. He scrambled out of the back seat and around to the driver's side, then worked with Rod trying to get him out of the car. Junior knew with every breath that he needed to get leverage on the open vessel within seconds or it would be too late.

Rod was staying composed through great concentration. He had learned in a First Aid class how critical it was to keep calm so that the heart did not race, and to keep a wound of this magnitude above the heart. So Rod continued to speak in those calm southern-like tones and encourage Junior. As Junior slid Rod towards the pavement by the driver door Rod's legs were rubber. Junior's hands, now covered with his friend's blood, were sticking to everything. Rod slid to the ground leaning against the car. Junior immediately found the space he needed to apply pressure to the neck.

"Use all the muscle you got, Junior. You can't press me too hard, buddy."

Junior, his left hand flattening the wadded up shirt against the neck wound and his right hand gripping Rod's left shoulder, squeezed his friend with every fiber of his being. Junior was not only using muscle to stop the bleeding, he was praying. "God, please don't let Rod die."

Another friend, Gary Patrick, was flagged down by Samoa. He pulled his orange pickup truck close by. After a couple of seconds of questions about what to do, together the boys awkwardly loaded

Rod onto the wooden bed of the truck so they could rush him to the campus emergency room.

As they rolled the short distance to the school hospital Rod had no idea if he would see the light of the next day, let alone walk again.

They passed the area where the school mascot, Butch the cougar, was kept. Rod had taken the name "Butch" as a sign when Mike Walker first walked him onto the playing field. Butch had been his brother's nickname. Somehow it seemed that Butch was there with him through his days qualifying for the team. And Butch was with him now. Butch had always protected Rod, stood up for him, kept him from trouble, and once again here he was.

As they got to the emergency room door at Pullman Memorial Hospital Rod was wondering if he would ever see his mom, dad, and brother Chris again.

The emergency room doctor took a longtime to arrive. Fortunately, Junior's pressure and prayers had indeed stopped the bleeding. After the examination Rod looked up at the doctor who was studying an x-ray of the neck. There it was. Even Rod could see the 29-grain bullet in that huge medical transparency. Rod had thought stopping the bleeding was a good sign and so he asked with a light-hearted tone, "Well doc, am I gonna live?"

Without any change of expression, his eyes still examining the x-ray, the doctor answered, "I don't know. It's too soon to tell."

Rod swallowed hard. Did he hear that right? Is this guy for real? He was too young to die. But then so was Rick. He thought they'd be discussing whether he would walk again. Now that question's value was moot. Was this his destiny? Dead at twenty-one! Too short to make the high school football team, too short to get the attention of any pretty girl, and finally he had made it to the big time and was about to taste all the good things life had to offer, and his life was too short to give him the reward he worked so hard for? And this because of the smallest bullet made, used to shoot varmints, a 29-grain round: a small round that became lethal?

These questions rifled through his thoughts in a millisecond. Then, without missing a beat he asked, "Can you bring a phone, please? I better call my folks."

It was a long wait that afternoon, waiting for night to fall so that Rod Retherford could then wait again till morning to find out if he would see the next sunrise. At this point one more day was everything.

1.

It was one o'clock in the afternoon when a couple of football team members crashed through the doors to Bohler Gym, screeched to a halt then blurted out, "Junior Tupuola shot Rod Retherford!" These words reverberated off the hardwood floors and wrapped themselves around every stunned molecule in this cavernous space.

There was total silence as Walden spun around in shock. Was it possible that another tragedy had struck his Cougar family? Was this a continuation of the horrible event that began last season, his first year with Washington State?

During fall training camp of 1979, the third day to be exact, a junior defensive tackle from Tacoma was doing his first practice in a night session. Walden thought of big and lovable Hayward "Spud" Harris as one of his kids. There had been eligibility questions when Spud arrived on campus, so the third day of practice was his first on the field.

Walden's kids were dressed in shorts and helmets that evening, prepared for a reaction drill. They had just finished their warm up and stretch, now they were scheduled for agility training.

Spud finished his first drill and walked to the end of the line, getting back in the cue with his buddies. He had not even broken a sweat yet. No contact or stress in this drill, it was more about mind work.

Right there, in front of all his teammates, Spud Harris collapsed. Coaches were on him in an instant pulling his helmet off, giving him mouth-to-mouth and pounding on his chest to restart his still heart.

This effort was to no avail. It was painfully evident that Spud had hit the ground dead. The autopsy never gave any answers and so his death remains one of life's mysteries for all who witnessed Spud's last breath, and for his family. Hayward Harris' time had come and no one could change his destiny. Unfortunately, yet understandably, his death took a toll on all his teammates. For the continuation of that season he was dearly missed.

But, on this September afternoon Coach Walden's Washington State University Cougar athletic program was struck by another dark cloud that had just announced itself like a clap of lightning. This was not the black cloud the coach and players had witnessed on a Sunday morning, May 18th of that year, when Mount St. Helens erupted.

On that day the earth shook as an earthquake measuring 5.1 on the Richter scale struck the state of Washington. The north face of St. Helens, a tall symmetrical mountain, collapsed in a massive rock debris avalanche. More than two hundred thirty square miles of forest was blown down or buried beneath volcanic ash. At the same time, a mushroom-shaped column of ash rose thousands of feet skyward and drifted downwind, turning day into night as dark, gray ash fell over eastern Washington and beyond. The eruption lasted nine hours, but Mount St. Helens and the surrounding landscape were dramatically changed within moments.

The wall of black that overtook the entire southern sky of the state literally snowed ash that accumulated to a depth of several feet. Instead, the dark cloud that landed on Jim Walden this day was one of personal tragedy. Another Cougar player might die.

The doctor had informed Rod that they were incapable of handling an emergency of this magnitude and had ordered an ambulance to rush him to Spokane, the nearest city with a hospital capable of dealing with this trauma. Spokane had been alerted and Rod knew that meant at least ninety more minutes before specialists could put their years of training to work in hope of saving a life, and maybe even giving him legs again. One miracle at a time, thank you.

After dialing his parents' phone number, the nurse held the phone to Rod's ear. As it rang he wondered what to say?

His mother's voice was still in his ears as he thought, "Had mom and dad not suffered enough for one lifetime?" And his little brother—the worry of this was not something he wished for Chris.

Rod had come to understand that people go their own way in times such as this. Survival mode. In the aftermath of the loss of a child sometimes parents will withstand the anguish. Most times too much of the grief manifests in ugly words and actions that memory will never release.

Rod and Chris had come home many an afternoon to discover their dad sprawled on the old easy chair with his empty glass barely balanced, the television filling the air with nonstop gibberish. The family trash business was faltering. If the boys had not taken the truck out on its route and dumped those often maggot infested cans by hand, the family would have totally collapsed.

Betty found the alternate road and went closer to God after losing Rick. This angered Jim. In fact he forbad her from going to church. He was foul-mouthed about it and cursed the heavens openly. However, Betty was an anchor for this family. Somehow she understood that there was purpose in all things, even in Rick's untimely death or her husband's brutish, though understandable reaction to the loss.

As the mother she is and was then, she provided everything she could to keep life in what would be thought of as normal for Chris. Why should he suffer at the foot of all this torment? She had seen him through the four years leading into high school while the post-Rick suffering filled almost every hour at home.

Sunday would arrive and Betty Retherford wanted to join her friends in church and pray. And though it was against the will of her husband, she finally managed to find her way to the last pew each week. Somehow, not stepping to the front of the church was a way of complying in part with Jim's demand. It might have seemed to some that she did not feel worthy to step that close to the rail. With such sorrow and tormented thought she may have found that her misplaced guilt gave her something to lean on and through it she held a sense of personal responsibility for Rick's loss, even though there would be no sane mortal logic that could render that judgment. Betty knew the Lord was the answer to her questions, self-doubts, and prayers.

Jessie Elliott, a lifelong friend that anyone would deem a blessing, so wanted to comfort Betty. She would see the tears streaming as Betty openly, yet silently, wept in that lonely last row of the church. Jessie understood the grief, never overstepped, but always encouraged Betty to sit with her family up front.

"I can't. He doesn't want me to," Betty would explain. Jessie may have understood the breadth of that statement as no one else could. Betty was in a way submitting to Jim's demand, but more likely through her pain she was suspecting that more within her needed self-examination before her Lord would receive her. Yes, she believed in an all-forgiving God. But this was her life and she needed to come to grips with all of it before she would be worthy of the foot of the altar.

It was months later, after tens and tens of Sunday services and many invitations to sit with the Elliotts that Betty acquiesced. It was a long walk down that center isle, but it was the shortest distance to emotional relief. Now, she might ask herself why she waited so long. Betty, always the rock for her family, understood the value of time. Like all things as old as granite, passing time was a given. It may bring torment but it also has a way to bring healing.

When Rod had heard that his mom had taken this step in church he knew it was a beginning of life again for her. She told him about it privately over the kitchen table on a weekend during the 1979 school year. He had come home from Treasure Valley Community College for a visit with the family.

The two-year school was in a small town on the eastern edge of Oregon. On a good weather day it was about three hour's drive from campus to John Day following state highway 26. The road cut its way over the beautiful Blue Mountains and dropped into the valley that cradles John Day. This was the ancient ground of the famous and fierce Paiute, Chief Paulina. A century before this was hostile territory to trespass. The Chief's curse on the settlers continued in the form of icy winter roads that occasionally lay claim to unsuspecting victims.

Rod and Betty had the quiet of the house for a good heart-to-heart that afternoon. It was a great sense of relief that came over him as he heard his mom speak about being in church, praying, finding peace. All the while she spoke he began to notice how many cigarettes she was smoking with her coffee. What had been a moderate twenty-year habit was now almost chain smoking. But that was a fleeting thought. To see his mom coming back to life gave Rod a sense of the light beyond this tunnel.

In that sterile hospital room Rod listened to the phone ring, then heard his mom answer. That voice in itself was a comfort in this moment of uncertainty.

"Hello."

"Hey mom."

"Hi Rod. How's my boy?"

He hesitated for a moment. "I'm okay." He took a second to finish masking the lie. "Is dad home?"

"No. Your dad got himself a job on an oilrig in Oklahoma. He went down there a few days ago."

The sanitation business, the boys called it what it was to them, garbage hauling, had failed during the tormented years following Rick's death.

Jim blaming God, repeatedly asking what good had it served to believe in the Almighty? His oldest son's tombstone answered that question for him, the bottle and the Darvon took care of the rest. Like many fathers, Jim had lived his life through his firstborn son. And it was Rick and Rod who many a day rolled through the streets of John Day in the garbage truck, helping the old man cover the work load. When Rod was in high school some of those trashcans weighed as much as he did.

Rod was glad to know that his dad was working again. Oklahoma is a long way from John Day but work for Jim was a sign of progress.

"Mom, there's been an accident. I don't want you to worry cause I'm going to be fine. But I think you might want to drive up this way and be with me."

"What happened, son?"

"I been shot. It was an accident and I'm okay. The school hospital isn't prepared for this so they are sending me up to Spokane. We're leaving here now, so maybe you should drive straight to Spokane."

Rod was trying to soft peddle the possibly tragic consequences of the news. He really didn't know answers to all the questions that might have come from her. Fortunately, Betty did not reel them out of her mind but rather elected to get off the phone, call Jim in Oklahoma, gather up Chris and start for Spokane.

For Rod, he had spoken a truth to his mom while at the same time instinctively protecting his family from more worry than absolutely necessary. The last thing that should happen in this circumstance was a highway accident that resulted from his mom being so panicked about another son dying. And, the horrible bleeding had stopped, Rod was breathing, his thoughts were clear, somehow he could not bring himself to accept that the grim reaper was really waiting in the wings.

As Coach Walden wheeled into the emergency room at Pullman Memorial, there sat Junior, flanked by Samoa Samoa and Gary Patrick plus a few other boys. Junior was as white as the boards on a picket fence, his eyes wide from the shock and red from the tears.

The doctor was at the nurse's station and recognized the coach.

"Doctor, tell me about Rod Retherford?" Jim said this less as a question but more as a demand.

"Coach, we've ordered an ambulance to transport him to Spokane. We're not equipped for such trauma."

"Is he going to live?"

"I really don't know. The good thing is the bleeding stopped so that immediate crisis has been averted."

"I want to see him." Again, this was not a request—it was an order.

Coach Walden was greatly relieved to see that Rod was conscious and the head of the bed was elevated so he appeared to be sitting up.

"Hey cowboy, you trying to scare us to death?" He said that with a confident grin, yet a worried brow. To Jim, Rod was a "Good old boy." There couldn't be a warmer compliment paid to a young guy from rural America.

"Hi coach. Sorry for the trouble I'm causing everyone."

Walden heard those blameless words and zeroed in on Rod with his intense eyes. "Son, you were on the wrong side of something. I don't think you need to be sorry."

"It was an accident—my fault as much as anyone's. It sure wasn't Junior's fault and you gotta make sure he understands that." It was evident that Rod was more concerned about the ones that fall victim to the wake of a disaster than he was himself. And this was reason number one for God's plan to take Rick from this world to another. Jim Walden did not know this subtle fact only because he was not privy to the Retherford family history.

But Rod was beginning to live in a stratum of life that was greater than he had previously occupied. Jim did know that this cowboy, pale from the loss of blood, bandaged like a soldier fresh from battle, was generous in his heart and soul. And that is why Rod Retherford earned "Cowboy" as a title in Jim's vernacular.

"They're taking you to Spokane son. Those folks up there will know what to do." The coach was nodding his head confidently. He too had to believe in the positive. What point would there be in anything else?

For Rod, having the coach stand beside him expressing his positive thoughts was even more certification and reason for real hope.

To Jim Walden the big Samoan, Junior Tupuola, was "Dennis the Menace" each day, and truly lovable in those same moments. For anyone unfamiliar with "Dennis," he was and is the main and beloved cartoon character of that title, having a penchant for mischief. He was brought to life through the late Hank Ketcham's syndicated newspaper comic strip. Like Dennis, Junior was always getting into trouble. While a tremendous football player, over the course of his Cougar years Junior was booted from the team yearly for a variety of minor infractions, none of which were any big deals. Nonetheless, these offenses could not be passed over because a precedent for undue tolerance would be established. But each time Walden would kick Junior off the team, he would miss him so much that he would invite him back.

Junior also had a way with the girls. It was his dancing. Yes, every girl in school wanted to dance with Junior Tupuola. Needless to say, that led to more trouble. He did the Michael Jackson moonwalk better than the superstar himself. He was smooth, agile, confident, fun loving, tireless—all attributes you would hope for in a football player.

The "Junior Alert" was devised out of frustration. The coach would put the alert into motion when he could sense that it was about time for another Junior screw-up. Walden would tell everyone to remind Junior that Coach was just around the corner. Maybe the effort stopped some of what might have happened.

When redemption was earned those big sad Samoan eyes would melt the coach each time Junior would come into his office and apologize. And each time Junior would swear trouble would never happen again, and the Coach would wisely say, "Yes it will, Junior."

"No, never again."

"Yes, Junior, it will happen again." And then Coach laughed, adding, "That's just the way it is with you."

"Okay, maybe it will happen again." The big Samoan's acknowledgement was polished off by his plunking down in the chair, his meat-cleaver sized hands turning palms up in a gesture that said, "I am who I am." But he also knew his good fortune here because unlike a lot of adults, Coach Walden appreciated the heart in Junior.

This time Junior rightfully anticipated the worst for his actions. He had held the pistol that placed Rod on death's threshold. But for the moment he was oblivious to Coach Walden standing in front of him. Junior was transfixed in a stare at the white hospital corridor.

Hands clasped, fingers interlocked, knuckles white from the

intensity of his grip, Junior was mumbling a prayer over and over. "God, please don't let Rod die. Please God, don't let Rod die." His hands were still stained in crimson and his grip was as powerful as it had been when the artery needed smothering.

Only Junior could see the face in the bright white light of the hall. He was staring into Christ's eyes. Junior had been raised in a devout Christian home. For him this was no hallucination. Christ was looking upon him with understanding. And Junior heard the Lord ask, "Do you have anything to say to me, son?"

"Please God, I'm so sorry. Let Rod live."

Coach Walden could recognize that Junior was in a dialog with an apparition. He made out the words and offered a response. "It's going to be okay, Junior."

Junior now could see the faces of his mom and dad, and his loving grandmother standing in the center of their family hut on American Samoa, in the village of Ili Ili. Behind her, offering encouraging faces were his two aunts and several of his cousins.

"Calm down, son. Rod is going to be okay," Walden said again as he leaned in and placed his hand on Junior's shoulder.

Junior looked up and then Walden's comforting eyes came into focus. "What's going on? What just happened?" Those big Samoan eyes were begging to understand.

"Rod's going to live, Junior. You need to calm yourself, son."

"The gun. It went off in my hand. I didn't mean for anything to happen, coach."

"I know that, Junior. I know. It was an accident." And then he added the most important words. "Rod's not holding it against you."

Junior began to cry again. This time it was relief in hearing that his friend would be there for another day. Tears of relief are good things. He would have no way of knowing what Rod faced if he survived. But the mere words being spoken by Coach Walden gave the big guy the chance to breathe.

In the quiet of the hospital room while Rod waited for the ambulance to transport him, he kept hearing the echo of something said four years before by his rodeo friend since age thirteen, Joe Sturza. Joe always attracted lots of listeners when telling his stories. Most of the tales were pretty funny. But now and again he would get on a serious point.

At that time Rod was riding rodeo on tuition waivers for Treasure Valley College in Ontario, Oregon. He had walked up to Joe as the cowboy finished tightening the cinch on his saddle. A couple of riders Rod's age, were talking to Joe. One was particularly proud of a Smith and Wesson *Model 19* .357 in his hand. As Rod walked up he heard the boy talking about the power of the pistol. Joe turned to the boy, rein in hand.

"You know what they say?" Joe asked.

The boy was all ears.

"A bullet always speaks the truth."

The boy thought about what Joe had just said, then asked, "What does that mean?"

Rod knew Joe's meaning but was curious how his friend would explain it.

Joe took a second, turned his head and spit some chew by the fence rail, and then responded. "It goes where it was intended to go. So, my friend, point that pistol where you intend the bullet to go. And it will speak the truth."

Joe pulled the rein and his horse stepped off with him. He winked at Rod giving him a classic Joe Sturza grin.

Rod walked off with Joe leaving the boys to ponder the advice.

2.

The palette the sun created for the sky as nightfall approached was a combination of apricot and lavender fuchsia. The warm light bathed the western face of the slope as the ambulance aimed its way north, parting the rolling wheat fields alongside highway 195.

Strapped into the gurney Rod had a view towards this miraculous heavenly moment. The sedative administered minutes earlier seemed to open his mind to celestial thought. He was contemplating that light warming his eyes. With deliberation he calculated time. He had recently learned the light coming from that ball of fire in the center of our universe, some 90 million miles away, was traveling towards us at the speed of just about 186,000 miles per second. His professor had explained that what light we see from the sun was created about seven minutes before we see it, and that meant that looking at light we were actually seeing into the past. That day he left the lecture realizing that stars millions of light years away from earth are views to the history of the universe.

And now he wondered if there was a way to step back in time? Many nights he had dreamt of flying, not in a plane, but Rod Retherford raising his arms and flying. Back home in earlier years his dreams had him climbing on the kitchen countertop and taking flight throughout the house. Releasing himself from the grip of earthly concerns—the weight of his life, then feeling free to move through space was for certain something that had propelled him to Washington State University. If only he could reverse time to a couple of healthy and promising hours earlier. But if he could do that why not go back six years and help Rick on that fateful day?

As happens everyday, people who love one another feel the full range of emotion. The brothers Retherford, young men with cowboy dreams, always helped each other in all things. At the rodeo they always assisted the other in the chutes as the brother took a seat atop equestrian or bovine dynamite.

That June 1974 day Rod and Rick got in a fight. In hindsight the argument's catalyst was forgotten, as is generally the case. Some petty squabble had led to the momentary decision by Rod not to help Rick onto that bronc he was about to ride. He left that task for Rick's friends who were nearby.

In later years Rod was wise enough to know that the practical result of his being at the chutes to help would not have changed the bizarre sequence of events. To this day no one understands how or why that horse, the name was Headlights, turned and kicked like it did. On that 29th day of June he watched Rick's ride from the other side of the arena.

Marvin Gibbs, a contemporary of Rick's, also a cowboy, drove Rod to the hospital in Bend, Oregon, all the while hoping that Rick would keep breathing. On the way there not much was said. Later Marvin would say, "I seen thousands of saddle bronc rides. Never seen or heard anything like that. Horses'll buck riders off overhead or sideways. Headlights bucked Rick off his right shoulder but Rick tumbled forward, his motion continuing in a summersault that threw Rick's head back in the air after he hit the ground. Headlights kicked again at the exact moment that Rick's head was rotating from the summersault. The horse's hooves connected with Rick's skull. It was loud contact between a rear hoof and Rick's head, like the cracking, shattering sound of a pro baseball bat connecting with a 98 mile per hour fast ball, that was heard across the rodeo grounds."

Brent Maddox, also competing that day, watched in slow motion not believing his eyes, asking himself the shocking question, "Is he dead?" Joe Sturza was in the chute, reign in hand, and scheduled next after Rick. Joe was the ultimate jokester and fun loving cowboy, never without a glib comment. For the first time in his young life he was without words.

Everyday since Rick's final one Rod replayed those last minutes. To back up time right now, hell, whatever the consequence, Rod would do it so as to have a chance to change history.

Rod looked at the attendant riding beside him. This was another days work, another ride to a hospital he thought. Rod had been injured many times in the Rodeo but never had reason to be taken to the hospital. Cowboys get hurt. Cowboys bandage themselves up and get right back into the chute. Rod was not the type to look for the timeouts, halftimes, or the stopping of the clock. Like those one-ton bulls who want to get the day over with so they can get away from all that human noise, Rod wanted this day to be over so he could get on with life, if there was any left for him.

That pistol in his car, a .22 caliber long barrel varmint handgun, had put him there. Its soft 29-grain round would have left the barrel at a velocity of about twelve hundred feet per second. Rod knew he would not be having these or any mortal thoughts had the pistol been of any higher caliber. And even though his life was still in question he also knew that the slightest change in the position of the gun could have killed him on the spot. Maybe he was reaching for the positive with this thought, but what else could he do.

Junior Tupuola and Samoa Samoa had jumped into Rod's car after the morning practice to head up the hill to the training table for noontime chow. The long practices were beginning to define a good team. And with Rod's great news of full-ride status, he was no longer on the outer edge of it. He was going the distance with his brother Cougars.

The ride up the hill would take three minutes. But Junior felt something under his seat as soon as he got in the car. Rod, being a guy accustomed to ranch life, having helped his dad with his livestock for years and having come to Pullman from John Day, forgot he was carrying the loaded varmint pistol in the back of his car.

Junior reached down to pick up whatever he felt under him. He laid the pistol in his hand in disbelief. Junior had never seen a pistol in person. He had no experience with firearms at all. The design of the pistol resembled the Colt .45 of the Old West. To Junior it was a curiosity. Little did he realize that the way it was resting in his big hand put his trigger-finger against the very thing it shouldn't be touching.

And so Junior Tupuola raised the pistol up in a gesture to ask the question, "Hey Rod, is this gun loaded?"

"Loaded," was still forming in Junior's mouth as the pistol

discharged its 29-grain load. That copper-plated bullet, traveling at twelve hundred feet per second as it left the barrel, found its target within eighteen inches. Fortunately, the bullet first had to pass through the muscle mass that Rod had developed in his shoulders during hours of disciplined weight training. That path slowed the object of death before it exited the upper portion of Rod's right shoulder, then continued to his neck.

After smashing through Rod's carotid artery the bullet came to rest in his vertebral column, also known as the Cervical Vertebrae. Nerves are like an electrical wire that facilitates the smooth, high-speed transmission of messages. Information in the nervous system is carried by brief electrical impulses that are conducted away from the body of the nerve cell to a muscle or organ. At the point of contact, or synapse, the information is carried across the gap between cells by neurotransmitters. The Central Nervous System has two-way communication. Nerve fibers either relay messages to the brain to communicate sensory stimuli, or they relay messages away from the brain to the body's tissues and organs.

Between cervical vertebrae C4 and C5 and a miniscule distance from the spinal cord, that thin, tubular bundle of nerves that is an extension of the central nervous system from the brain, protected and enclosed by the bony vertebral column, the copper-plated tiny missile from Rod's varmint pistol had stopped. The slightest change in Junior's movements as the weapon discharged would probably have taken Rod's life in that instant.

The white smoke cleared and the Dodge Colt stalled as Rod lost the motor skill to control the accelerator-peddle or manage the clutch. The deafening sound was the first shock and its effect caused Samoa Samoa to defensively bailout of the passenger door. The blood pumping from one of Rod's paired carotid arteries was the second shock, and this was what Junior saw through the smoke. Hysteria and prayer began in that moment.

As the Colt shuttered to a stop Rod realized what had just happened. He had lost his sense of feeling. He knew he was shot but could feel no pain. In the next few heartbeats the image of the last deer he dropped flashed in his memory. Even though he hunted for food, not for just the adventure of it, and though he used every part of the deer in honor of its life, the image in his mind of standing over the majestic buck, burned through his thoughts. It was not the sight of its large eyes motionless as he walked up to his trophy coming up in this momentary flash of memory, it was the second step the deer took after being struck by the rifle shot. This was the step in which the animal faltered as its central nervous system shut down and its legs collapsed. The death was deliberate. Yes, it was a part of managing a healthy population of these wild animals. It was legal. But in this moment, as a victim of a gunshot, Rod was struggling in his subconscious with the fact that he was the one who had decided to end the life of that creature.

As darkness overtook the highway Rod very much wanted to speak to Junior. This accident was not his Samoan friend's fault. Rod hoped he understood that. And, even in this altered state of mind under the influence of the hospital administered sedative, Rod knew there was no way anyone could reverse time. The gun had gone off, that sound heard throughout the adjoining dorms. For some it would be heard for a long time. The inquisitive had watched in stunned silence as friends rallied to place Rod on the bed of Gary Patrick's pickup. And now an ambulance ride was bringing him to Spokane, to a hospital and thankfully not the morgue.

3.

Betty pushed the family sedan as hard as she dare, running along the shoreline of the Columbia River. She had stopped in Hermiston to fill the tank before crossing the river at Umatilla and entering Washington. She was a third of the way to her oldest living son.

Vic, the boy's "Uncle Tats" from their dad's side of the family, joined them and relieved Betty with the driving. Chris had turned eighteen and was a senior. There was not much they had to say along the first part of the drive. Chris had brought his NERF basketball and was passing the miles silently tossing it from hand to hand. He was internalizing a lot with these words repeating in his thoughts, "This is really going to suck if I lose my other brother."

Betty spent most of the trip praying silently. Chris certainly understood that these were hours that might turn to either darkness or light. Prayer was the means his mom had as they closed the distance to Spokane and he gave her the space she needed.

At Chris' age he should not have understood so much. But he

was bathed in experience from the cruelty of Rick's death, and so destiny was in his thoughts. The matter of his remaining brother's life was now in the hands of providence.

For Uncle Tats this was all too familiar. He had been through the aftermath of Rick's death. He remembered Rick lying on the couch in Tat's apartment saying, "Uncle Tats, if I die—it'll be with my boots on." Fortunately Rick's last breath was taken doing something he loved, and with his boots on. And now Rod's life was threatened doing something he loved.

Betty had reached Jim in Oklahoma by phone. There was not much to say in that call. He immediately made arrangements to fly to Spokane where Tats, Betty and Chris would meet him.

For Jim, the flight was insulated from the immediacy and panic Betty felt on the ground. Glimpsing pockets of light cradled by the earth thirty thousand feet below allowed his anxiety to lift. The flight was lightly booked so Jim had the row to himself. He declined the beverage service, turned off his reading light and drifted into uncontrolled reflection.

Anger is stimulated by pain. Jim's pain began long ago, well before his handsome firstborn son was taken from this earth. As his boys went through school and the demands on learning increased, Jim had masked his inadequacy from them. Where he could participate and shine in the eyes of his kids was sports. Jim loved football and had played one year of college football in Eastern Oregon. He had been pushed through high school because of his athletic ability. He knew the fine points of tackling and taught his boys early on how to wrap-up a runner and bring him down.

Jim was fierce in his support for his boys in athletics. And, as every child should be blessed to have, he was truly a constant source of encouragement. "You can do it." "You will do this, no one will stop you." How many times he had said those words? This father of three boys so wanted to free them from the earthly boundaries that had stopped him, but he had not realized this limitation for himself in years now past.

When asked by strangers, "What do you do, Mr. Retherford?", his reply would be, "I'm a businessman and a family man." True words. But his business, the Retherford Sanitation Company, was now a failure. Since the days when Rod had left for Treasure Valley College Jim had no one to pickup the slack when his depression paralyzed him. And yes, in his heart he was a family man, but in the aftermath of Rick's death he was barely there in mind. In this hour, flying north, Jim knew that without Betty's steady motherly presence his boy Chris would have been denied any warmth to develop in.

As an adult, Jim was basically illiterate. He could barely read. Without Betty covering for him he would never have pulled anything off in business. Yes, he had graduated from high school, had attended one year of college, but he could not read. No one would have assumed this. For this man, to watch his boys with pride as they developed raised the specter of harsh conflict due to his inability to interpret their homework or answer the questions put in front of his eyes to read. This discord manifested itself in anger. And when Rick died it unleashed years of internalized disappointment with himself, and denial about his own father.

Jim was named after his dad, James Retherford, Senior. Jim worshiped his dad. He wanted to emulate his dad. James, Jr. bought his dad's sanitation service company to keep it in the family and continue an effort to be just like his dad. Like father like son, both had foul mouths. Jim so admired James, Sr. that he had no opinions he could express other than his father's. His entire adult life James, Sr. was not a church going man and other than using the Lord's name in vain, he did not talk about God—that was until near the ending days of his life. However, James, Sr. openly held great disdain for a John Day minister who had taken advantage of his generosity.

The circumstance that provoked this dislike happened just after the minister's church had burned to the ground. James, Sr. donated one of his large trucks to the church for the clean up from the fire. The Retherford sanitation company had the trash contract with the church and James, Sr. felt the community and his company should offer to help in any way possible. However, this gracious act was totally overlooked when the minister later decided to award a contract to a competitor of James, Sr., thus taking business away from the Retherford family. The minister had sold out for a slightly cheaper bid and the senior Retherford would never forget it.

Understandably, this gross oversight made James, Sr. very angry so he called the minister and expressed, in no uncertain terms, his fury. "You call yourself a Christian minister, a man of God? You think you are an example to your congregation by selling my company out? That's about as un-Christian as it gets."

"Mr. Retherford, you dare call me un-Christian. I'll tell you that's making me pretty darn hot under the collar," the minister said with a lot of attitude.

"Well, I tell you what, minister. You just step outside your door and I'll be right over and cool you off."

Had the minister accepted that invitation James, Sr. would have certainly "cooled him off." Fortunately, the confrontation ended with the phone call.

A year before Senior's death Jim, Jr. was at his dad's home when the family asked Minister Milo Frankie to visit the elder Retherford. This occurred during the years after Rick's death, when James, Jr. blamed God for taking his oldest son. On the day of Milo Frankie's visit James, Jr. heard his dad, the man he had worshipped for a lifetime, answer a strong question put forth by the minister who preached the word of God.

"Do you, James Albert Retherford, truly believe in God?"

Without hesitation, and with extraordinary conviction, Senior answered, "Yes! I do believe in God."

A year later when James, Sr. was in his last day of this life, and he was comatose, non-responsive to all, James, Jr. sat alone with his dad. He was trying to speak with him when a nurse said, "Mr. Retherford, you're dad can't hear you. You need to understand that."

James, Jr. politely acknowledged the nurse as she went on with her rounds. He noticed the time was 2:50PM. Senior's head and back were slightly elevated, his eyes were closed, he seemed very peaceful to Jim. With the nurse gone and quiet returning to the room Jim placed his right hand over his dad's joined hands. At this point Jim was studying the face of the man he worshiped. Memories of his childhood flowed through his consciousness like warm sand passing through his fingers. Time was passing, his father was passing, and Jim could feel that he was, himself, transcending his mortal thoughts. An unexplainable dimension had taken hold of Jim. He did not resist the experience and would only later realize that one-hour passed quietly while father and son held hands in a strong gesture of love and emotional support.

Jim looked up at the clock and it was 3:50PM. An hour had passed in a minute, it seemed. His dad was labored in his breathing at this point. Jim joined his two hands around his dad's hands. "Dad, I love you so much." Jim took a deep breath. He dropped his head and said to himself, "If only I had this moment sooner."

Then, looking at his dad's hands he added this affirmation. "No one could have asked for a better dad. I will love you for eternity."

James, Sr. took a very deep breath and Jim looked up at him. Tears were running from James, Sr.'s eyes. Jim realized that his dad had heard him. Another deep breath was to be James, Sr.'s last. Jim openly wept as he felt life leave those strong hands he was holding. Yes it was painful to realize that in this life he would never again have the comfort of his mortal dad. But Jim's tears were as much an emotional release of four years of hatred. Jim realized that God had given these two men a final instant of life to share.

This moment, years into life, was the moment of second birth for James, Jr. He entered a realm of thought that would now allow him to develop, to take his worldly experience and turn it into a vital life. But as with all things in nature, he was in an embryonic moment and time would have to nurture this seed. He would later realize that he had communed with God in that moment.

Albert Einstein made the statement "God did not play dice with the universe." In those words that extraordinary man of physical science, who had given birth to the most advanced understanding of the controlling laws of the cosmos, confirmed his belief in God. He knew that the brilliant simplicity of those controlling mathematical laws of science could not be serendipitous. Jim was now given freedom to discover and in so, acknowledge God.

Through years of torment Jim was unknowingly preparing to be born again. "Born again", a phrase overused in our daily vernacular, is one of vital meaning throughout all cultures.

"Except man be born again, he cannot see the kingdom of God," so the bible quotes St. John. In Hinduism the word is Dwija, and it actually translates to "Twice Born."

Such enlightenment had arrived not one moment too soon in Jim's life. And, for the Retherford family it was the same. Jim had tried to kill himself before. His failings, his son's death, his spiritual void, all of existence led to the question, "What purpose did any of life serve?" Through his devotion to his dad he had unknowingly denied himself his own thought.

Adding to the emotional complication was an innocent prescription for Darvon years earlier. It was intended to relieve the pain from arthritis that had begun to grip Jim's knees. In the aftermath of Rick's death a couple of Darvon a day had increased in number to three hundred a month. The swelling in Jim's knees was such that he could barely manage the six-foot walk from his bedroom to the bathroom in the morning hours. Relief of pain through a licensed drug is intended to make life manageable. When the human spirit is crushed before it ever develops its resilience to the events that destroy the weaker, then it becomes ground ripe for destruction.

Jim's torment had built to a point where he purposely caught his foot in a stirrup and allowed himself to fall from his horse and be dragged, hoping for an end. Certainly no accident, but an attempt, a design to die in a manner identical to his grandfather's death by trailing behind a horse and dragged until life was crushed from his head.

Earlier attempts had caused James, Sr. to ask Rod to be with Jim when he went to work. Those were painful long hours for both men. Rod was torn though. On one hand he wanted to help his father but on the other he deserved a life of his own. A family drowning in pain was not an environment likely to spawn growth. Going onto school to further his education was something that no one could challenge, and in so doing Rod was able to take his first step to a future.

As the 737 crossed the Rockies covering 500 miles every hour Jim was in a former time. He could see Rod jumping in his child's spring suspended rocking horse. His tiny, developing legs were too powerful for his age. Rod would lift that rocker right off the ground. Seeing this exhibition of strength Jim had a premonition that this boy of his would grow to be an athlete. In the years that followed he would work with his sons teaching them what he could from his football years and his love of the game. The boys were so fearless their tackles were hard enough to break helmets. One can easily understand how any coach that was less than supportive of the Retherford boys would receive this dad's wrath.

Rod was close to Spokane, influences of the city starting to show. "How much longer till we're there?" he asked the attendant.

"Ten minutes. Hang in there, buddy."

"Oh, you can count on that," he replied.

Rod looked down at his hands, resting on his belly. The fingers of both hands were cupped. He asked himself, "Are they useless?" This was a healthy question because his mind had gone past "Will I see tomorrow?" Rod figured if he was going to die from this injury it would have already happened.

Suddenly in a motion he might have missed had he not been staring, the index finger of his left hand snapped open as if he were flicking a fly off his wrist.

"Hot damn!" Rod said that with excitement. "My finger just moved."

The attendant looked at him. "That could be a good sign."

"Could be? Are you kidding me, man? That is a sign. If that finger will move we'll just see about the rest of me." Rod said this with a widening grin and look of enthusiasm.

Then Rod concentrated on that same finger. He pushed that impulse, that nerve transmitted command to his finger. The signal seemed to move in slow motion, the information passing to his index finger. Suddenly it flicked again, just like it did before. Rod was wearing a big time grin. He looked up at the attendant who had watched and was now grinning with his patient.

"Hot Damn. I got me some fingers. The rest of me is coming."

4.

Spokane's Deaconess Hospital had completed a battery of tests, examinations, and x-rays by the time Jim, Betty, Tats, and Chris arrived. Rod was sitting up in bed. His left arm and hand were coming back to use. He had also managed to walk, with assistance from nurses. However, his right-arm showed no sign of movement.

The attending physician and the neurology specialists found Rod's condition to be amazing. By all medical standards he should be dead. He had suffered tremendous damage in the immediate area where the bullet entered his cerebral vertebrae. The idea of surgery to remove the coffee bean sized object was tabled since there was greater fear of either creating further nerve damage or rupturing an artery and causing his death. Rod was stable with one functioning branch of his carotid artery, even though that was all that was oxygenating his brain.

A second chance at life was at hand. Rod agreed completely

with the recommendation to leave well enough alone. For the family this news, to see Rod have the ability to walk and have use of one of his arms, was an answer to prayers and a powerful lift of their spirits.

When Rod managed to put one foot in front of the other and step into the hospital corridor, pushing his rolling I.V. stand, then take up a game of NERF basketball with Chris, Betty cried in relief as Jim thanked the Good Lord out loud. She believed that Jim having begun joining her at church services, his having found God, was part of the reason Rod was physically able to join Chris in that simple game. And typical of Rod's determination he was using that arm that wouldn't work, making it swing like a pendulum so he could toss the ball to the NERF basket that Chris had hung on a door.

Later, in a private moment, Jim would say, "Son, you know God has healed the arthritis. And the loss of your brother is something I accept. I'm praying for you to have a complete recovery."

Rod still had a difficult time with the idea his dad was a praying man. It was so far from his years of experience. But he was seeing what he was seeing. He knew that his mom was at peace, and certainly it was evident that Jim was no longer hitting the alcohol or the Darvon. His face and eyes no longer had that puffy look.

"Dad, I appreciate your prayers. I really am glad to know that you and mom are seeing things the same way. Life's got to be a bunch better at home, especially for Chris."

Uncle Tats hung back with Rod when the others went for some food. Rod loved his uncle. He was the salt of the earth. He had great memories of the days growing up and visiting with his Uncle.

"Hey Uncle Tats, you remember when you used to put that belt around your chest so's I could ride you?"

"Son, you were too young to remember that now. You weren't but about four, maybe five when that was happening." He laughed. "You loved that didn't you? Climbing up on your old uncle's back, grabbing onto my belt while I tried to buck you off!"

"And you never did." Rod said this with a big shit eatin' grin.

"Yeah, you would dig your tender little heels into my ribs and hold on for every twist and turn I could muster."

"Jack saw that and knew you'd be in the rodeo." Jim was "Jack" to his family. "Then there was the day you decided to stand on the basketball. You had unbelievable balance. I still can't believe it. No wonder you could ride a bull."

Acknowledgement of Rod's unique athletic ability had helped him survive the question of his size over the earlier years. While he loved football as a youngster he found individual sports to be loads of fun because it was in those that he always received praise from his peers. The acceptance he wanted in team sports was another matter. Early on Rod had taken to wrestling and it was very rewarding. He wrestled kids his size and his athletic ability and strength per pound gave him a major advantage. He also applied his skills to track and field. This was a personal challenge since he could measure his improvements by both time and distance.

Rod's favorite was rodeo. This was a test of his skill combined with overcoming fear. When strapped to a bucking horse or a bull he knew that he lived or died in eight seconds. The enormous power of the animal that he would straddle, realizing that he was trying to keep control of something that was at least ten times heavier and that had its own mind about the ride, was the ultimate turn on. The rush he would feel as all that caged energy breathing and shifting under him in chutes exploded into the arena, was not to be matched.

Rod's conversation with Tats had all the warm memories, and the grins were plenty, but the mood turned serious.

"Rod, you have taken on your athletics with unbelievable drive. When Rick was still here you didn't seem to have a lot to prove. You were still pretty small and riding with the disadvantage of being so light."

"Yeah, at one-hundred-twenty pounds you ain't much more that a gnat on the back of one of them old bulls," Rod said.

"Wasn't long after Rick's accident that you became reckless. You seemed to have something to prove."

"Well Uncle Tats, my big brother wasn't there anymore. And it was time for people to take me serious. And I was angry. I put that anger into those rides. I made sure that everybody knew—that I proved that Rod Retherford was worthy of being taken seriously."

Rod reached over for the plastic water cup. Tats instinctively reached to help him but stopped, knowing that Rod was going to do this whole thing himself. That boy would find his own way, his own speed, his own drive.

"You just don't know what it feels like to be told over and over by coaches and other kids that you are too small. They would laugh at me for trying to compete—until I beat their ass at whatever it was. Maybe being started in school one year early was good and bad. I was always one year younger than anyone in my grade. Think about it, Uncle Tats. I was a whopping four feet eleven inches tall and eighty-two pounds soaking wet on my first day of high school."

Rod paused for minute remembering some of those times. He got a little misty-eyed then added, "They weren't saying that shit when I won the western states championship for bull-riding."

"Two years in a row," Tats added. "Rod, you overcome some huge odds along the way."

"You been a believer in me all along, Uncle Tats. Can't tell you how much that's meant."

Tats walked over to the window. This was getting pretty emotional and he needed to pause for a second.

Rod kept talking. "Even this past year I was dealing with things from the outside looking in. You know, I was playing football for the Cougars, but because I was a walk-on the equipment manager wouldn't give me a locker. They reserve those for the guys on scholarship. They put the walk-on's in the general school population, with the rest of the student-body. And I couldn't use the team weight room either. I had to use the equipment in the gym. Talk about feeling like an outsider, a less than."

Tats was amazed at that news. "Why?"

"I don't know that I could explain why. All's I know if it weren't for Ken Woody, the coach and recruiter that talked to me at Treasure Valley and invited me to walk-on to WSU, I'd never have seen the inside of the team weight room or locker room. I told Coach Woody about my locker and how it made me feel. He had no idea and was really embarrassed. He took me to the strength coach, Ray Naworol, and that condition changed."

Tats gave Rod something to chew on. "Rod, you been fighting your way through life, always too short, too small, an underdog, an outsider, younger than your classmates. That's the stuff that made you a great competitor then and now. And right about now that may be the reason you'll be walking out of this hospital and onto who knows whatever is next."

"Yeah, I think about that from time to time, Uncle Tats. I guess there's lessons and blessin's in all sorts of things. But they sure ain't no fun to live through," Rod added.

"But you're figuring it out. How many guys did you beat out to win that full-ride scholarship? How many guys make it onto a PAC 10 school football team? How many win western states championships riding bulls or busting broncs? And bless Rick's soul, how many young men survive the loss of a big brother? You have come through the wars, boy. For you it's just part of your life, and another day at the barn. This kind of stuff stops people all the time. And here you are sitting up talking to me in a hospital bed moving on from a bullet that still sits in your neck."

Rod was watching his uncle, listening to his life play back as if it was being read from a newspaper story. This was just the first part. All the struggles that had come before were preparing him.

"You know, you're right Uncle Tats. Since it's all been a fight to prove myself, everything I do is like game day. You know, practice is a good example. To me it's not practice. It's a game day. I hit as hard, I run as hard, I get as mentally prepared as I can."

"Well, what you've overcome has always been a big factor." Tats scratched the side of his face then added. "But you're a lucky one."

"How do you figure that?" Rod asked.

"Your dad and your mom have always given you boys lots of encouragement. It's been a constant, even in the dark days that Jack went through after Rick. Plenty a times I heard him encourage Chris just like he always did with you and Rick."

Tats moved up close to the bed. Rod reached for another sip of water, managing that cup pretty well.

"All this adversity has made you tough. All that encouragement has given you confidence. I'm not taking anything away from how hard you worked for your goals, I'm just saying it's everything put together that makes you who you are."

Tats took Rod's hand, clasped it firmly. "We're all pulling for you. Now, I'm going out for some air. See you in a bit."

Before Rod said anything Tats turned and walked from the room. About that time a pretty nurse walked in and handed Rod a menu of dinner choices to check off. His eyes were following her as she continued her quick steps to the next room. One of his doctors walked in at that moment taking notice of Rod's interest in the nurse.

The doctor commented, "Good to see you are returning to normal."

"Hey doc. No harm in looking at the sights."

"How you feeling?" This was a very routine question.

"With my fingers, again," Rod said. That got a smirk from the M.D.

"Watch this." Rod picked up the water cup and took a drink then looked over at him with that grin.

"That's really encouraging." The doctor picked up Rod's chart and studied it for a moment. Then he replaced it on the foot of the bed.

"Your vitals are all excellent." He did a quick examination of Rod's eyes, having him follow a penlight from side to side.

"Can you lift your left arm?" he asked.

Rod complied slowly with a degree of concentration. "It's like it weighs more."

"And, how about the right arm?"

"Nothing happens." Rod looked down, concentrated on the arm, but nothing. "What do you think the chances are that I'll get it back?"

"You know, when I first examined you, if you'd asked me the chances that you would be walking around here twelve hours after being admitted, I would have said—maybe twenty percent. You should be really happy with where you are.

Rod asked the logical question. "What about the bullet? Will you cut it out of me?"

"If we attempt that you will most likely bleed to death. There is too much damage. Look, only time and therapy will give us more answers. You may never get that arm and shoulder back, or maybe you'll get some of it. I wouldn't count on it. At this point, be thankful you're talking to me."

"I understand." But what really was going through his thoughts was, "Here we go again. Someone is telling me I can't do something." Rod took a second and then, "How long are you keeping me?" At this point Rod wanted out. He had something to figure out, something to fix, and a football program he was determined to be a part of.

"I'll see you in the morning. If your vitals are the same, you'll probably be released tomorrow."

The doctor went on about his rounds. Rod sat there contemplating the past twenty-four hours. The entire experience was happening, but in some way he was feeling like stepping outside of his body to look around.

As much as Rod believed anything he knew that Rick was in that room watching out for him. Frankly, Rick was probably in Rod's car and made certain that the bullet stopped. In that realization Rod knew that there was yet another reason, another purpose, for Rick being taken to the next life.

In the middle of the night, despite the sedatives and the quiet, Rod woke out of deep sleep to the sound of a gunshot. It was almost deafening. The accident was replaying vividly in his dreams for the first time. As Rod came out of this nightmare in the dimly lit room he realized he was sweat drenched from the very alive experience. He had no way to anticipate that this was to be a nightly experience for many months to come.

5.

Earlier in the summer of 1980 before Rod went up to Pullman to walk-on to the Cougar team he had dated a pretty, athletic girl in his hometown. Patti Wright was one of the four Wright kids. She had two sisters and a younger brother. Patti's dad, Jackie Wright, had been a professional rodeo bareback rider in the RCA, Rodeo Cowboys Association. Rod being a rodeo competitor in the junior rodeo had made a point of getting to know Jackie, and through that contact had met Patti. Being a good-old-boy, Rod used to pick up Scott, Patti's one brother, when he was too young to drive and take him to the rodeo when Rod was competing.

Patti was a triple threat athlete, volleyball, track, and, basketball being her disciplines. Her healthy attitude was attractive to Rod. He and Patti dated, shared some intimate moments as young people will do on summer nights, but the relationship was too new to turn to any serious conversations about a future. Rod went off to WSU to begin his university experience, whatever and whomever that might bring to his life.

When Patti heard that Rod was shot and was in the Spokane hospital, she decided to visit him. Accompanied by her sister, Marty, Patti drove to Spokane. Rod was surprised and as well, pleased to see her. For a young guy who had come so close to death, who had never been the one to get the girls during his high school years, to have a pretty hometown filly who he had only dated for a few weeks make the effort to drive up to Spokane for the singular purpose being to see him, was a validation that he was worth some real effort.

Indeed, Rod's vitals were good that next day in Spokane. The doctor prescribed therapy and he was released, his right arm in a sling. It was all matter-of-fact. The world goes on whether you live or die. If Rod had been rolled out of the hospital as a quadriplegic life for everyone else would have continued. Or if a vehicle from the morgue had rolled up to carry him away, all those people outside his immediate family would have continued on.

Rod had not had reason to think about this reality in such blunt terms. The depression and anger that followed Rick's death was too overwhelming. But at this point he was seeing more clearly. He was also beginning to understand that time here is measured not by us, but by something that is probably predetermined and totally out of our control.

Whatever happens, the sun is coming up every morning in the east and setting every afternoon in the west. What we do as individuals is not going to change that fact. When we're down the world is not going to stop and wait for us to pick our butts back up. And when we do something that measures as great, it too will be a fleeting moment. Make a serious mistake and it may cost your life, or screw up in the eyes of the law and you may spend a lot of life wishing otherwise while counting days, months, and years.

So, Jim returned to Oklahoma; Betty, Chris, and Tats, drove back to John Day. Patti had volunteered to drive Rod home since he needed to pick up his car from Pullman, and Marty could drive herself home to DuBois, Idaho from there. Patti would drive Rod home to John Day in the Colt parked at Pullman.

The stop in Pullman was brief. School had not started yet so the campus was still pretty much a ghost town other than the football pre season training camp. They found Rod's Colt parked in the lot a few feet from the scene of the accident. She volunteered to wipe the bloodstains off the upholstery. Rod thought about helping but her motherly instinct insisted that she would get the car ready for them.

He walked across the street to say hello to the coaches and found a few of them meeting. Jim Walden stopped the session and gave Rod a big welcome. While it was a relief to see him walking, the undercurrent was his arm in the sling. And the unspoken question when they learned that the bullet was still in his neck was, how fragile is he?

Rod was as positive as a guy can be telling the coaches he'd see them when school started. The encouragement offered collectively was sincere. As Rod left the room the coaches went back into play diagrams and season planning for their first game that was coming up in days.

Rod walked back toward the Colt a little surprised that there was not more attention paid to him. He was having an internal argument and ultimately dropped the question. He told Patti how glad the coaches were to see him standing in the room. This was a truth.

As they started on the trek back to John Day Rod kept thinking about life moving on. It does not wait for anyone, any circumstance.

Those fifty-two hostages held captive since November 4, 1979 in the US Embassy in Iran by the Khomeini government were living this realization with each day of their seemingly endless ordeal. On the other hand, Rod was free to pursue his life. Everyday is a gift. How many times had he and do we all hear that when growing up. It takes on meaning when life is just about snatched from us, right before our eyes.

The ride home took them east seven miles to Moscow, Idaho, home of the University of Idaho. Then they traveled south across the White Bird pass. This is the eastern edge of the Palouose region. It is a major wheat-producing agricultural area situated near the Oregon Trail.

The highway that cut across the White Bird pass follows along part of the route the Nez Perce Indians took in a desperate attempt to flee the US Cavalry and reach Canada. That was only one century earlier, in the summer of 1877.

Rod asked Patti if she knew about this history. Learning she did not, he proceeded to share the story of a small band led by Chief Joseph, who had refused to be placed on a reservation.

"And why should they have believed anything offered at that point? Hell, repeated treaties had been broken. So this small group of Nez Perce warriors lost patience and killed some settlers who had been less than hospitable with them. And, fearing retribution, the band fled through Idaho seeking refuge in Canada, going right over this pass. The US Army and a bunch of volunteers chased them, and eventually caught them after fifteen hundred miles and three and a half months."

Rod and Patti had passed quite a few historical markers along the switchback and S curved roadway. Rod was trying his best to keep his mind actively engaged so to avoid the nausea that was wanting to grab him. Finally, he could no longer handle the driving. He had Patti make an abrupt stop and he spent about ten minutes puking.

Fortunately, the zigzag portion of the highway ended soon after his upheaval. However, from that point on, he was nauseous until he placed his legs on terra firma in John Day.

She had politely thanked him for the history lesson on the Nez Perce right after they hit the bottom of the pass but asked no further questions. Rod knew that his interest in that history was peculiar and certainly did not expect everyone to share his curiosity. So he moved on with thoughts that passed the time, but not before recognizing that stories of the underdog, like Chief Joseph and his people, really intrigued him. Knowing that others overcame great odds in life convinced Rod that the end result of his life was in his hands.

During the drive across the valley Patti asked him about his plans.

"I'm getting healed and go back to school. This ain't gonna stop me. What else would I do?"

"But, hun, you can't be overdoing it," she interjected.

"I ain't overdoing anything. But I am going back to school." It had not been thirty-five hours since the accident. Rod had recovered his legs, his left arm, and he was sure his right arm and shoulder was soon to be healed, despite the warning from the doctor.

During the winter before he had worked out daily on the free weights with Max Hull. Max was a self-taught trainer. He had lifted weights in the Air Force where he first competed in the sport. He was about Rod's height and was a self-motivated guy. Rod respected the hell out of him and this was very mutual. Max could bench-press over four hundred pounds!

During the eight weeks of winter Rod worked out like a crazy man. He put on twenty pounds and added two inches to his arms in that short period. When Rod started with Max he could bench-press one hundred forty-five pounds and had twelve and a quarter inch arms. Eight weeks later he was bench-pressing one hundred eighty-five pounds and had fourteen and a quarter inch arms. By no means did Rod think this was big, but there was no doubt in his mind that he was bigger and more capable of making the cut to play Division 1-A football in the PAC 10.

Discipline was the key word. Of course he wanted to accomplish this task of developing himself. He was walking onto Washington State University and nothing was going to stand between him and this opportunity. Rod and Max would do workouts together each day. Max was the manager of the local supermarket otherwise he would have spent all day, everyday, working with Rod.

During the summer that followed, after Rod had walked on for spring training and made the team, he had again returned home needing weight training. But now he required more than what he had available at home. Rod decided to request use of the weight room at Grant Union. He met with the superintendent at the high school and informed him that he had made the team at Washington State University and really needed to workout for the summer.

The superintendent's response was quick. "We're not letting anyone in the gym during the summer."

"But sir, I'm representing our high school as an athlete in Division 1 football. If I don't train I won't be able to compete."

Unmoved the school official added, "You're just another tax paying citizen, not a student. If I let you in here, I'll have to open the doors to everyone in town."

Rod realized this was a door that would never open through

bureaucracy's channels. But, there was another way. Rod remembered that the janitors entered the school building daily through doors that were very near the old weight room. During the early morning hours of the next six weeks Rod would sneak in the building through doors left unlocked by the janitorial staff. A few yards down the hall he would make his way to the weight room. Once inside he would crack open a window, place a twig in the jamb—preventing the window from locking, then sneak out. After night would fall he could climb into the room through the window. Once inside Rod would place a flashlight in the corner so light would not betray him to the world outside, and then he would do his workout.

For the next six weeks Rod followed this routine in order to weight train, all the while fearing that he might be caught and arrested. Seeking another solution, he drove thirty miles down the John Day River to the small town of Dayville. There he spoke with the local high school football coach, Skip Enscore. Skip had read about Rod making the team and was really proud of him.

After the congratulations Rod put his problem on the table. "Skip, can I come down here to lift? The people at Grant Union won't let me in."

Skip was baffled on both counts. Then he asked, "You're gonna drive all the way down here, everyday?"

"Skip, I gotta do what I gotta do."

Skip pondered the situation for a moment and then said, "Come with me. Lets go to Mr. Thorn's house. He's the school superintendent."

Rod was introduced to Mr. Thorn and Skip first told the superintendent about Rod's great accomplishment, then he explained the dilemma about weight training.

Mr. Thorn was a quiet man. He listened to all of what was explained and after congratulating Rod, simply said, "Follow me to the high school."

At the school Mr. Thorn had Rod back his pickup truck to the gym doors. Then, this quiet man along with Skip, began grabbing weights and loading the truck. That afternoon all of the high school's weight equipment was loaded into Rod's truck.

When they finished Thorn shook Rod's hand. He simply said, "Bring the equipment back at the end of summer when you're done with it. Good luck to you."

As Rod drove home to his Mom and Dad's house, he almost cried at the generosity that this stranger showed him. He setup the weights in the yard, and was able to train for the balance of the summer. The spirit of this gift was to influence Rod from that moment forward.

Rod loved sunset while on the road. It usually occurred after a day of rodeo when he was heading for the proverbial barn and a well-earned night's rest. His best memories included Rick as they would float big brother's sixteenth birthday gift down the highway. Two cowboys, Rod the younger at fourteen riding shotgun in a 1966 electric blue Ford Galaxy 500 that Betty and Jim bought well used for six hundred dollars. To Rod, life could not be any better. For Rick, having one of them sweet rodeo girls in his arms was pretty darn good. But that was just another night. His hours traveling with his little brother were the stuff of lifelong companionship. These two knew they would share all the great moments of their lives.

Rodeo ran in the family genes. Betty's cousin, John Quintana, who lived in Redmond, Oregon, won the world Bull Riding championship riding in the PRCA. The Retherford boys grew up on rodeo. Rod, with John's younger brother, Rex Quintana, traveled together a lot during their teenage years, riding bulls.

Rod was returning home to a safe environment. His mom loved to cook for him. He would get healed, healthy, and back to what all his hard work had earned him. There was only the matter of his arm and shoulder, he thought. How quickly he was forgetting about that 29-grain bullet that sat within a mere fraction of a millimeter of his the spinal chord.

6.

John Day, like all towns and cities, has certain qualities fixed within it forever. The town grew out of the 1862 Gold Rush era and was a ranching and farming community until the World War II years when logging and saw milling became the principal industry.

As Patti passed the Hudspeth Saw Mill and Pond on the outskirts of town Rod remembered his first job after high school. Working on the pond further cut the cloth that made Rod such a dedicated asset for a football team. Experience with hard work and dealing with discomfort, getting past what stops many, were simply a part of life.

His first day at Hudspeth Rod was baptized, literally. He became a pond monkey. For a mill worker that's where it begins, and that's at the bottom of the food chain, just one step above night watchman. Rod was sent onto the pond by his foreman to break a landing jam. He could see the huge logs tangled right where the foreman was pointing. And Rod could just hear him over the sounds coming from the steam-operated saws, belts, and conveyors that made up the machinery within the mill.

"Yeah, it's a bitch. They dumped six truckloads last night." Then the foreman pointed to a pole, a "short-pole" to some, about the size and length of a shovel handle. On the lower portion there was a lower-bar like the hinged part of an arm. The lower-bar had a hook at the bottom with spikes that could grab onto a log.

The foreman continued, "You take that old fool-killer and get hold of the log out front, the one that's under the water."

Rod was looking way out at that log wondering just how he was getting there as he continued to listen to instructions.

"You just twist her tail until you free up that jam. When the jam gives way look out. That pond's gonna come alive, son. Them underwater logs'll burst to the surface while all the logs in the middle starta rolling. That's when you better watch yer step. You fall between them logs and you could become hamburger. If you're taking a plunge make sure you come out on the end of a log."

Rod had figured out that he would be walking on top of those logs and certainly did not want to ask the question to confirm anything, lest he become the fool for asking. He had enough experience with kids making fun of his size or being denied along the way. So, he made his way out to the center of the pond, dancing across the big logs. That amazing balance of his once again came into action. And, Rod was mechanical enough to get the idea of the short-pole and how it worked. He did free up the jam.

But, just as predicted, those middle logs began rolling as the jam cleared. Rod was out on the end of the whole litter of big floaters and now had to make it to shore. He sized-up the situation, made a quick decision about his route to safety, then began hopping and leaping his way to where he started from. Had he been a running back in training this would have been effective if not unusual training. He almost made it, but as happens to every person in a pond monkey job, Rod fell in. But he had listened and knew not to try to come up along their sides. On the shore and in the mill no one seemed to pay much attention. It was a part of the daily routine, one that Rod became very familiar with in the months that ensued.

Rod would eventually build a little seniority, moving inside the mill to the tail saw, a treasured warmer environment during the winter. However, he was also pulling green chain—a tough outside job, but it beat the heck out of being a pond monkey. Pulling green chain meant you were working with that heavy green rough lumber that exited the sawmill by way of the green chain, and was pulled by hand into stacks. Green lumber is heavy since it still has moisture. And some of it was as big as two inches by two feet by twenty-four feet in length. At the end of each week, he'd collect his pay and head out to rodeo. No time off for this cowboy's body.

Rod looked at the familiar sites as they passed the bowling alley just before hitting the main commercial area. The town was named for the nearby John Day River. While it was then a community that was ninety-five percent white, the 1879 Census listed 960 whites and 2,468 Chinese miners in the gold fields of Eastern Oregon.

The town had been named for a Virginian member of the 1811 Astor-Hunt party. Rod knew the history of John Day well from his time at the mill, his time in the garbage truck with his dad, and from being a kid that grew up there.

A trading post built in the area in the 1860s along the Dalles Military Road was purchased in 1887 by two of the immigrants, Lung On and Ing Hay. They converted the trading post into a clinic, general store, and social center for the local community. The local Chinese could worship, smoke opium, socialize in their native language, and gamble. Right after Rod graduated from high school that building was converted into a museum and state heritage site now called the Kam Wah Chung & Co. Museum.

Rod was one of the first to visit the museum. There he learned that John Day was a hunter from the backwoods of Virginia and had arrived in Oregon at about forty years of age. Rod had noted that he was tall, six feet two inches tall. It had been his boast that in his younger days nothing could hurt or daunt him, but he had lived too fast and injured his constitution by excesses. This was a life experience that Rod could relate to.

John Day's adventures were many and included a journey where he and Ramsay Crooks, a fellow pioneer, were attacked by Indians, robbed, and left naked near the mouth of the Mau Mau River, thirty miles east of The Dalles. After the attack the two men started back to the friendly Walla Walla country when they met an immigrant party going to Astoria. The two men joined this party and reached Astoria in early May, 1812. People started calling the Mau Mau River "John Day River" because he was attacked there. Within a very few years, maps changed the name to John Day, and then a valley, two cities, and the fossil beds took on the name of the river. Rod had further read that John Day became "deranged" and attempted suicide during one of his later expeditions.

Whatever the case might have been at the end of his life it was clear that John Day must have been quite a man because so much in the area was named after him including a large dam on the Columbia River.

And so, Rod Retherford was home, even though it was to be a short visit. School was starting in one week and Rod planned on being there. Depression began setting in though, since with each passing day his right-arm and shoulder would not respond.

Rod watched Washington State University's first game of the season with Chris in the living room. He was unusually silent through the game. Finally, he walked out of the room saying, "I should be there."

7.

Rod walked out of his parents home to be alone on that afternoon. It was the weekend after Labor Day, one week after the gunshot. Watching his Cougars play football on television, knowing that were it not for the 29-grain round in his neck he would have been one of the athletes on the field, was really pissing him off.

Sitting on blocks in front of the house, where it had been parked since that day in June of 1974, was Rick's Galaxy 500. Rod walked alongside the big sedan remembering how it looked in better times when that electric blue was shimmering. In the autumn light of this afternoon he remembered the pride beaming on Rick's face when he rolled up from the tire store after having polished mag wheels and baby-moon hubcaps along with those big ol' rear tires installed. Lots of extra hours working in town at the Ye Ol' Castle restaurant washing dishes had paid for those absolute necessities.

Summer of 1973 was the best memory for Rod because the two older Retherford brothers were living the life. On the weekends when they would head off to catch up to the junior rodeo circuit they had been competing in for years, they would hope to do it without the parents, just two cowboys on the road.

Rick had an old guitar case carefully placed in that big-ol' trunk of the Galaxy. He lined the case with Visqueen, the brand name for polyethylene plastic opaque sheeting used in the construction trade. Then Rick would fill the case with ice and beers. The boys would toss their gear in the car, climb in and head out. As soon as they were clear of the town, out would come the cowboy accessories: Beechnut chew in one side of their mouths, a Swisher Sweet Cigar in the other, and a can of beer between their legs. Rod's legs could barely reach the floorboards but in his mind he was as tall as his big brother.

Motor idling, positions set, country music station at the ready, the boys would look at each other grinning like Cheshire cats, then with rehearsed synchronization out would flow, "Swisher Sweets, God Damn it!" With that they were off.

Rick would get that sedan rolling so fast going across the flats that the speedometer would be pegged at one hundred-twenty miles per hour. She'd just float down the country roads. Cowboys on the highway, they were rolling as free as tumbleweeds. Sometimes they would have the other member of their dynamic trio joining them. Mitch Gregg was a cowboy too and the bass player in Rick's band.

The band, *The Continental Divide,* played its first gig in 1971 as a brother duo at the Anchor Club, a John Day restaurant, bar, and motel. Rick was the lead guitarist and vocalist, Rod played drums. It was not long before Mitch joined them as a rhythm guitarist and backup vocalist. Their repertoire covered tunes of the day from the greats like Merle Haggard, Johnny Cash, and Leroy Van Dyke, and what are now classics including John Fogerty's *Proud Mary* from his band Creedence Clearwater Revival, Kris Kristofferson's *Me and Bobbie McGee* which made rock and roll history when Janis Joplin recorded it in 1971, and Bob Dylan's song from the motion picture "Pat Garrett & Billy the Kid," "Knockin' on Heaven's Door."

Being a lead singer and guitarist certainly has its advantages with the ladies. Rick had no end to the opportunities. This was the one difficult reality of that time for "too-short" Rod. Barely over five feet he just could not get the attention of the girls. But Rick was darn near six feet. He was handsome, seemed shy, which always was attractive, could sing and play, and was a cowboy with his own wheels to boot.

The Continental Divide was booked for rodeo dances in addition to the local John Day dates. One of those times was in Hermiston, a town in the northeast corner of Oregon. Calvin Clark, who rode in the PRCA in those years, was like an older brother to Rick and Rod. During a treasured no-parents weekend rodeo, Calvin rolled into the Hermiston Motel around 1:30 in the morning with a sweet country peach by his side and found Rod sitting on the front step of the motel, by himself. Rick's Galaxy 500 was clearly parked in front of their room.

"What the heck you doing sitting out here, boy?"

"I don't know," Rod answered.

"Where's Rick?"

Rod tossed his eyes back towards the room. "He's got him a girl in there."

Calvin studied the situation for a minute. "Well how long's he been in there with her?"

"About an hour and half," Rod answered.

"Hell, if that boy ain't succeeded by now, he's never gonna."

Calvin rolled right to the door. Rod followed him, a grin coming up on his face. Calvin did not hesitate to step up, take a quick listen to the room, and then hammered on the hollow door with his big fist. "Time to go to bed, Rick. Send her home."

After a long hesitation Rick responded with a little southern drawl like Rod's, "Okay!"

And after the girl went home as was always the case, and whether Rick drove her or whether she was in the same motel, the brothers would have a good laugh about Calvin's antics, talk a little about the gig, maybe a little jawing about the day's rodeo and what was coming the next day, and then fall off to sleep.

They were gentlemen. Rick didn't brag about the girl or what he had done. Rod would learn to be the same way.

The next morning the brothers would be at the rodeo grounds for another day's competition. The events in junior rodeo included calf roping, bareback riding, saddle bronc riding, and calf riding, also team roping and bull riding.

Calf riding was and is the junior rodeo preparation for bull riding and it was Rod's favorite event. The calf was rigged in the chute like a bull, rigged with a bull rope and a flank strap, that's the strap around the rear of the animal. A calf usually will buck a little but they are mostly unpredictable. They may buck a little, a lot, none at all, or they may just run. The rider would hang on for all his worth and try to make eight seconds, the length of the ride.

In bareback bronc riding the horses were harnessed with rigging equipment that gave the rider a handle. Using a strong grip and a lot of arm and balance the rider had to immediately catch the rhythm of the horse as it left the chute, matching it to the riders spurring kick. As the bronc bucked up into the air, the cowboy would lift his feet, pulling his knees almost to his chin.

As the horse went up and over, then started back down, the rider straightened his legs bringing his spurs to the horse's neck just before the animal's forelegs hit the ground. It was this rhythm that revealed the skill of each contestant and still is to this day.

In saddle bronc riding as with the bareback riding event, the cowboy strived to match the rhythm of the horse to his own spur stroke. Balance was the greatest asset and the rider achieved this by lifting, not jerking, the braided rein attached to the halter. The ride was always unpredictable so the cowboy made the best he could with his rein—too long and he would not reach high enough to take up the slack, too short a grip and the rider would be yanked over the bronc's head to the ground. It was the combination of best grip, best rhythm, and best style that would lead to the best ride— and all of that was a natural for Rick.

Rod was a winner. He won the year buckle for the calf riding when he was twelve and thirteen-years-old. On the other hand, Rick was really good, consistent, yet never won a championship. He placed many times, being in the top six rides for his events. Bull riding was Rick's best event, however he really wanted to be a champion saddle bronc rider. It's only fitting that his last event was a saddle bronc competition.

Rick was very proud of all the buckles his little brother had won and continually encouraged Rod since he knew the too-short issue dogged him.

Jim Retherford brought his boys up to protect each other and their family. Being the oldest the weight of that responsibility landed squarely on Rick. If that meant going fisticuffs with a stranger, or a friend, so be it.

David Michael Liberty met Rick on David's second day in

John Day. His family had moved from Pendleton, Oregon and he wanted to make new friends. Sports offered the avenue and joining a baseball team would bring him in contact with kids his age.

Late in spring David walked on the baseball field where a game was in progress and asked about joining a team. He was introduced to Don Jones, the head of the area's Little League. Don said the team on the field right at that moment needed another player so he should meet their coach.

As David shook hands with Jim Retherford, he was surprised to hear, "Are you Bryson Liberty's boy?"

David nodded.

"He and I played football at Eastern Oregon together!" the coach explained.

David's stock suddenly went up in value and his chest puffed a little. Jim brought Rick over and introduced the boys. When Jim told Rick he had played football with David's dad, Rick was impressed.

In the months of the season that followed Rick and David became teammates, then friends. Overnighters at the Retherford house became a regular event. Rod and Chris were always hanging around with the older boys and so David got to know Rod. David also learned that Jim ruled with an iron fist and demanded his boys do their best and give life their all.

Over time Rick and David were teammates not only in baseball, but football, basketball, bowling, and swimming became part of their mutual experience. They spent so much time together they became brothers, for a while.

In their freshman year in high school the boys went down very different paths. Rick became a cowboy and David became a hippie. Opposite ends of the social spectrum in John Day and other parts of the country in the early 70's, and it still is.

But there was a day two years later when the fundamental Jim Retherford requirement of brotherly protection surfaced and hit David Liberty between the eyes. David Gibbs, a contemporary of Rod's, snatched one of Rod's cowboy boots for fun while the boys were at their lockers. It was all in jest but that singular boot flew out the front door of the PE locker room at the hand of David Gibbs.

The joke almost stopped there, but David Liberty happened to be in the vicinity when the boot landed. He decided to join in on the fun and took it a step further, tossing the boot out the front door into the parking lot.

The Retherford brothers spoke that evening. Rick did not say much when he heard the story. The next day Rick walked into Grant Union high school and headed directly to the locker area. David Liberty was just opening his locker when he felt a tap on his shoulder. He turned and was to only remember a flash of light before the pain of a busted lip came on. Rick had popped his old friend, now a hippie, but mostly someone who had messed with his little brother.

Pulling his hand from his injured face David Liberty saw a very intense Rick.

"Ow!" David was recoiling and still seeing bright light. He added, "Man, what did you do that for?"

Rick answered in a matter-of-fact tone, "I don't much appreciate your treatment of Rod. You disagree, we can take it outside right now."

David realized he had stepped over a line and deserved this notice. No way was he going to turn this into a fight, for it would have been on false premises. Rick had taught David a valuable lesson about brotherly love, protection, and more importantly, about violating sacred family ground.

Sadly, David Liberty and Rick never spoke after that. David's wife was at the rodeo the day Rick was killed. She has never forgotten the sound of that bronc striking Rick's head. That evening when she cried telling David about it they both acknowledged how much Rick had touched their lives, and now, that he made them very aware of their own mortality.

Ten years later David Liberty would visit Rick at his gravesite on a painful day after David's own child's interment. At Rick's headstone he had a conversation with Rick

"Sorry your young life was cut short, Rick." David stood there reading the words on Rick's headstone. "What would you be if you were still alive?" he wondered.

That gravestone above Rick is perched atop a hill that overlooks John Day, Oregon. It faces east and is warmed by the afternoon sun, that glorious time of day when those young cowboy brothers would roll down the highway heading for the barn.

"Rick" James Richard Retherford
February 3, 1957—June 29, 1974
"Cowboy on the Road
I'm a Rodeo cowboy and I'm always on the road.
I hit a hundred rodeos with a heavy load.
I'm gonna break my neck someday so I've been told.
But I'm a rodeo cowboy and I'm always on the road."

As the sun dropped below the western edge of the mountains Rod walked back into the house. He found his mom in the kitchen, ready to serve dinner. Without saying anything he put his arm around her and gave a most wanted hug. It was something that he needed to do for her, and for himself. After a good fifteen seconds he asked, "So, what's for dinner?"

"What do you think?" she replied, with a wry smile.

"Better be good," he said with a twinkle in his eyes.

Betty had prepared his favorite dinner: Chicken fried steak, creamed corn, and mashed potatoes. The family sat down for dinner, first saying a prayer for all: Jim in Oklahoma, Rick in the heavens, all their friends, the hostages in Iran and their families at home, but especially the Retherford family was grateful for the gift of Rod's presence at the dinner table.

8.

Rod arrived back in Pullman the day Washington State University began their fall 1980 session. He had been assigned a dorm room with a stranger. No more Mike Walker and the comfort of an established friendship. At this point life seemed pretty cold to Rod. This was a homecoming for him, but only the ballplayers had a sense of the meaning of his return to campus. And even with that they were consumed with their lives, moving forward with overwhelming schedules day to day.

The first thing Rod did was walk on the football stadium turf. It was quite a different feeling than the day Mike Walker took him on the field. This day, by himself and in the chilling air of the fall afternoon, with the bleachers empty and his right arm in a sling, the dream of playing before thousands of enthusiastic Cougs was hard to imagine.

Walking towards the coach's room he passed players. While they were all glad to see him, and some surprised by his appearance on campus, they had little time for him. Rod was getting the sense of being on the outside looking in. He could not get his mind around this. He was one of them. How many scrimmages? How many meals at the training tables? How many jokes? And suddenly the guys seem to barely know him. He was outside the cherished fraternity wanting back in.

While the coaches asked about his health and were clearly pleased to see him on his feet and back in school, there was no question that Rod was interrupting their preparation for practice and the upcoming game strategy discussion. Not being one to ignore circumstance, Rod moved on with his day. Maybe tomorrow would bring him an opportunity to have words of encouragement flow from the coaches. That was certainly not this day's experience.

Rod walked across campus toward his dorm. Passing pretty girls one after the next, none of them seeming to notice him, further put this lonesome cowboy at odds with his new life as an outsider. He remembered and longed for the feeling of pride that he had briefly owned on the day he and his teammates were introduced to the student body of WSU as their 1980 Cougar football team. What a day that was for the little kid from John Day.

UCLA was playing WSU's basketball team. Coach Walden who wanted the new guys on the team to feel the pride he was instilling in the program, arranged to introduce all the junior college scholarship recruits at this big hometown game. He specifically asked Rod Retherford to go with them, the only walk-on to receive the honor. Rod was being introduced at a game with UCLA? He could not believe this was happening. It was another one of the stupendous moments he felt as all of his past diminished into just that, the past. Earlier in the year Rod was living in the present. He could not wait for each day to begin. They were all the 4th of July. Every meal was a feast.

Coach Walden had taken Rod aside earlier in the day and told him to be there for the introduction at halftime. He wanted Rod to feel as much pride as the kids on scholarship. And so there he was, Rod Retherford, defensive back, standing shoulder to shoulder with PAC 10 star athletes.

Across that hardwood court his eyes locked onto a cheerleader at the same moment she had looked at him. This was no passing glance. He could feel the intensity of her look and it kept him transfixed on her.

Jann Arnold was from Hawaii and was beautiful, tan like the girls Rod had so often seen in photos of exotic faraway places, full of smiles, excitement, curves, flowing hair, every single female trait that the kid who sat on the steps of the Hermiston motel a few years earlier would never have imagined could be warming up his eyes, intentionally.

This was a great memory for Rod and important, for in his state of mind to think about such moments would possibly awaken his passion for challenge. He was feeling depression grip him. Remembering the night he met Jann was a good place to be in this moment.

It was after the basketball game that they first spoke. A local club in Moscow, Idaho, named Hose Apples was the place. The legal drinking age in that state was nineteen so the drive from Pullman, a mere seven miles, was nothing. Rod's roommate, Mike Walker, and Gary Tate, a running back for WSU, had made the drive with Rod. They were telegraphing their football team status by wearing football polo shirts and turf shoes.

Sharing a room with Mike, "Walk" to his buddies, was perfect for Rod. Walk introduced Rod to his friends and took him to some very cool parties. Rod really preferred going to the black parties because it was so much about the dancing and grooving. The white kid's parties were routine—breaking out the keg early and drinking until they were stupid.

Hose is where Rod had the confidence to walk up to Jann and asked her to dance. However, this was not before taking in the vision she was as she entered the club. She was wearing a sleeveless black jump suit with a V-cut neckline that plunged below her navel.

This was the disco era so they were moving to the Sugarhill Gang, who had introduced millions to the new hip-hop sound with their single "Rapper's Delight." Kool & the Gang's "Ladies' Night," and Chaka Khan's "I'm Every Woman" were at the center of that day's music scene. It was a broadening time for Rod and music that had cross-cultural appeal was a part of it all.

Jann accepted his invitation to the dance floor. He was a handsome guy, stout in both body and mind, so certainly not your average college kid looking to get laid.

When he took her to the dance floor what struck Jann almost immediately was that Rod was a gentleman. Being from the Islands she new nothing of the cowboy traditions. What she had experienced plenty of times were egocentric jocks, fresh on campus thinking that they were a gift to any woman. But Rod did not give her one of those all too familiar signs. He was not aggressive in any form. But she could certainly and undeniably feel that there was a lot of passion in that cowboy. The less he did the more she wanted to know him. That slow moving way, that deliberate and comforting southern sounding voice, it was the most appealing encounter she had at the university. Rod was the most humble, gentle, kind, and well-mannered man she had fallen for.

Their similar small town roots, yet from totally diverse cultures, gave them a further bond. Jann, the oldest of four, had gone to the University of Hawaii her freshman year. She longed to experience life on the mainland and when the opportunity came to transfer to Washington State University, that was her desire. It was not an easy accomplishment since she would be the first of the children in her family to not only leave home, but to leave the Islands.

Rod and Jann dated for the next month. The Cougar basketball team was playing with a lot of promise and entered NCAA tournament play. This took Jann on the road. In addition she was further along in school and 1980 was her last year at WSU. While the romance was fleeting it was seminal for both of them. She knew there would be no locker room talk about her, and they both knew this was not about another conquest. They had each experienced their first adult romance, and that promised something great for their futures.

That cold afternoon what Rod would have given to have Jann sit beside him? But she was thousands of miles away and in a different world of experience. They shared a memory. And then he thought, "Maybe it wouldn't be so good for her to see me now." Rod knew that his mind was in a different place then it had been months ago. Aside from the injury, he was not the same confident guy.

Rod's right arm was showing no sign of recovery. Moving around campus with a dead arm, trying to deal with books, opening doors, cutting food, just about everything in day to day activity, became a trial. But what gnawed at Rod was how he was ever going to get back on the football field.

Compounding the entire problem was the athletic scholarship that Rod was about to sign before the accident. Coach Walden had to explain to Rod that he was no longer eligible. This is not an easy thing to explain to someone who you want to encourage. Saying, "Hey son, you just lost your full-ride. Tough break, but that's life. But hang in there, there's lots of opportunities for guys who almost made it." Those were not the kind of words that would ever come out of Jim Walden. Yes, the coach was tough. His personal standard was high and he demanded the same from his staff.

Coach Walden had told his staff, "Trust is a big word with football players. Hell, that's a big word in anyone's world. But with these players, you can't lie to them. And, when they screw up, scream at them if you need to. Dress 'em down, whatever it takes to make the point. But make damn sure that before that kid leaves the field you sit down and talk to him, make sure he understands."

And so the coach wanted Rod Retherford, a good-old-boy for sure, who the coach found to be remarkable for the mere fact that he was standing in front of him within days after damn near dying, to understand. He could see self-pity was on the edge of setting in. But coaches don't have time to be a friend to their kids.

"You know Rod, you gotta understand something right now. That clock on the wall is ticking. Time is linear. We don't get to back it up. Your buddies who you were tackling two weeks ago are living under that clock. There's a finite number of minutes until their next game day. They are looking to me to get them ready. They don't have time to stop. Sure, I know they all feel bad for you. But they've got no time to dwell on it. And, I'm sure not going to let them.

"My job here is to coach a team that is going to face John Robinson's USC, Terry Donahue's UCLA, Roger Theder's CAL, Bill Walsh's Stanford, Rich Brooks' Oregon, and especially Don James' Huskies.

"Those kids have to be ready. Do you understand what I'm saying?"

Rod had been listening to words that in one sense seemed really harsh. But he knew they were spoken in truth. Rod also knew that he could not take being a passive member of the student body. His world had been defined through sports, through competition, through accomplishing the very things that people told him he could not do.

"Well coach, I do understand. And, I have decided to leave school. I'm going to go home and get healthy."

Walden immediately underscored the position. "Your scholarship will be here, waiting for you. You have two to get two." This meant he had two years of playing left that would earn him two years of tuition.

"I'm protecting that," Rod confirmed.

"You'll be welcome when you come back."

That following day Rod withdrew from his scholastic class schedule, packed his few things and said good-bye to the Washington State University campus. There was a way he would come back, but it was going to be on his terms not what he had experienced in this week.

Rod Retherford believed he would wear the crimson and grey jersey again. He believed he would run out on that field in front of tens of thousands of fans. He would give his heart and soul to the game he loved. He would do this not to be patted on the back or because of those fans, he would do this because it was his destiny. What anyone else did now was not his concern. And he realized that what he accomplished in his marked time on this earth was something of personal choice. Being alive now was the gift.

9.

Depression grips the spirit. It is an illness as potentially destructive as cancer. It takes lives in its path. It affects entire societies. History gives many examples and one of the most disturbing from the twentieth century is the collective depression of the German people after the defeat of their country in World War I. That condition gave birth to the power of a human embodiment of Satan named Adolph Hitler. His control of the minds of millions is recorded fact.

On the Threshold of Eternity, a 1890 Vincent van Gogh painting, is seen by some as symbolizing the despair and hopelessness felt in depression. Van Gogh himself suffered from clinical depression and committed suicide later that same year.

While "depression" is frequently used to illustrate a temporary decrease in mood thought of as "feeling blue", clinical depression is a serious illness that encompasses the body, mood, and thoughts that cannot simply be willed or wished away. It is often a disabling disease that affects a person's work, family and school life, sleeping and eating habits, general health and ability to enjoy life.

Depression can be a once in a lifetime event or have multiple recurrences, it can appear either gradually or suddenly, and either last for a few months or be a life-long disorder.

Clinical depression is usually treated by psychotherapy, antidepressants, or a combination of the two. Clinical depression may be a standalone issue having differing features in patients, or as part of a larger medical issue, such as in patients with bipolar disorder or chronic pain.

Attacking the individual mind, depression following tragedy is to be expected. But how much can one person deal with? For Rod, maybe another reason or purpose in Rick's early death was Rod learning to cope with whatever life threw at him. He had survived those earlier years that could have brought down his entire family. In a rural small town such as John Day, a family suffering depression had friends or the church to reach to for help. And to many, like Jim Retherford, acknowledging depression was a sign of weakness. This was beside the fact that there were no psychiatric practitioners easily available to them.

Arriving back from Pullman after dropping out of Washington State, and during those dark, cold days that arrive in fall, those sunlight starved weeks of winter that follow in John Day, Rod had little clear thought. He was not counting blessings. He was on the verge of falling back to earlier times after high school when marijuana and booze were the standard M.O. of his days.

Rod's first experience with weed was in 1976, his senior year of high school. An innocent visit to the Prairie Maid, the hamburger joint that was next door to Grant Union High School, was the place.

It is hard to believe that in his time a high school student would not have been exposed to marijuana in some form or fashion. But this day was to be Rod's first.

Hungry after school he had walked to the Prairie Maid and ordered a burger and fries at the window. There were a few picnic benches that sat on a grass shoulder next to the building and Rod decided to sit there. A former classmate of Rick's was finishing up his meal as Rod sat down. The two boys went through some idle chatter and then Rod saw the schoolmate strike a lighter and hold the flame over the top of a soda can, then draw air in from the drink opening at the can's top.

"What the heck's that?" Rod asked.

"It's a portable pipe. Want a hit?" The boy offered the can to Rod.

"A hit?" Rod had no clue what this was.

"Yeah. Marijuana. Try it. Takes the edge off."

Rod thought about it for a second. "Yeah, I'll give it a try."

The boy handed Rod the can and lighter. The can's side was slightly flattened from the pressure of a puncture from a pocketknife. A bud of grass was resting over the puncture.

"When you light it, draw the smoke in and hold it for a few seconds before you blow it out of your lungs."

Rod followed directions, took the can, raised the drink hole to his mouth, struck the lighter and then connected the flame to the weed. He drew it in deep. Since he was used to smoking the Swisher Sweets the smoke entering his lungs was not a new sensation. The buzz that hit him a minute later was.

That afternoon stop at the hamburger stand was a beginning to a cycle, using the blanket of this common recreational drug to cover his continued pain over life after Rick.

Fortunately, earlier that school year football had reentered Rod's life or he probably would never have tasted the sweetness of his brief encounter with PAC 10 football years later. High school football his senior year happened through the coincidence of being in the right place at the right time.

It was the summer before his senior days. Rod was enjoying an afternoon at the community park in John Day. The Gleason Pool was used during the summer for swim team practice and meets. It was a twenty-five meter pool with a ten-foot platform and three meter springboard at the deep end.

Rod had just completed a series of dives and flips off the springboard before taking a final jump from the platform. He was toweling dry when Don Jones, the longtime assistant coach at Grant Union high school, walked up. Don had been at the school for years. He had watched Rod play freshman football and compete as a wrestler.

Rod's freshman year had been promising for him with his love of athletics. He went out for football and made the team playing for a gangly coach by the name of Morgan Groath. He was new to Grant Union and John Day that year, 1972. As summer camp progressed towards the school year Coach Groath kept putting Rod in as a quarterback.

Rod could not understand why but never argued with the coach's decision to play him in that position though several times he asked himself, "What's with this coach? What is he thinking? I'm four feet eleven. I can't see over the linemen to what's happening down field."

Rod would take the snaps from center standing straight up since the center was much taller. The other position that he found himself playing was middle linebacker on defense. This was another shock. That would normally go to the biggest, fastest, most mobile athlete on the team.

Rod started at quarterback for their first game, also playing monster linebacker. His small-size thoughts would become overshadowed by enthusiasm and confidence. And, Jim and Betty were thrilled to see their boy being recognized for his skill.

On defense, Rod led the team in tackles. His fearless eighty-three pound frame went up against the biggest and best and no one got past him.

The football season ended and Rod went into wrestling. This is when he first encountered the varsity football coach who covered both sports. Size was not an issue and Rod went to the state championships, setting a new school record with the fastest pin. That pin ended Rod's match against a freshman from Burns High School. The Retherford record was now established at twelve seconds.

At the end of his freshman year Rod could not wait to get onto the sophomore experience. He still could not believe that in football he was an offensive starter, and on defense he led the team in tackles. This came along with his record in wrestling and a varsity team letter. Unfortunately the varsity football coach brought the thrill of Rod's first year crashing to the ground when he told him not to bother trying out for varsity football because he was too small.

As Coach Jones approached Rod at the pool he had no way of knowing that in Rod's junior year he did not need or want any rejection and therefore never considered going out for the football team, despite the fact that Don was then coaching. But the coach knew enough about Rod's ability, and was motivated by the chance meeting at the pool.

"Hi coach," Rod said in a respectful manner as Don walked up to him.

"Hey Rod. You're pretty agile on that diving board," Don commented.

"Yeah, that's a bunch of fun."

The coach then asked, "So how's your summer been?"

"Busy with rodeo, the usual stuff. Helping my dad with his business."

"So listen, we're starting summer training for football soon. Don't know if you know that I'm varsity coach this year."

"Congratulations, coach. That's got to be an improvement."

Don looked at Rod for a second and then asked, "You wanna play for me, join the team? I could, we could use you."

Rod was stunned. He could not believe that someone was asking him to play football. After his previous experiences with the former varsity coach telling Rod there was no way under any circumstance that he would play him, Rod almost could not speak.

Don finally asked again. "So, what do you think? Will you play?"

"Yes sir! I just can't believe someone is asking me to play. That's why I didn't answer you, coach. I was, speechless I guess."

That invitation, spawned by Don Jones needing all the recruits he could get, and certainly influenced by knowing that Rod Retherford had the heart and will to be a competitor, became a crucial time in Rod's development. Playing varsity football gave him experience that was sorely needed, and it also gave him the reason to be coached by Gene Winett.

Gene arrived at Grant Union to teach Physical Education a few years before. He was also appointed defensive back coach for the varsity football team. Having spent a few years in the US Navy where he had been a Fire Control Technician aboard the USS Piedmont, Gene had great experience to bring to the boys he was given to inspire through sports.

Being a small school, the Physical Education teachers would help out in all sports. Gene had witnessed the friction that existed between Rod and the former varsity football coach, who also coached the wrestling squad.

When Rod's senior season started and they were handing out equipment, assigning player numbers and the like, the preference was given to returning team members. Additionally, Rod being five feet and three inches and one hundred twenty-five pounds, he was the smallest guy on the varsity football team. When they got to Rod's equipment there were few things left that were not well used. He did manage to find a decent pair of pants since he was so small that no one had yet used his size.

But shoulder pads were a different matter. The high school had no shoulder pads small enough for him. And this fact was determined while the boys were gathered, receiving their gear."Retherford, here's what we got. Maybe you can make it work for you." The equipment manager was handing Rod a torn up set of pads that had been through many seasons and were well overdue for the junk pile.

Rod took the pads with both embarrassment and disbelief, turning beet red. There were a few unidentified giggles that added to the discomfort of the moment.

"You're so small that's the best we can do," the manager said as he turned away.

To the manager this was another day dealing with students. For Rod this was personal. It was an embarrassing moment that he wanted over. No more open discussions about how small he was, thank you.

He took the problem to the grade school and got equipment that fit him. In the best of circumstances he was still wearing inferior shoulder protection. Grade school kids are not hitting or tackling one hundred seventy-five pound running backs. But Rod would make up for what was missing with his determination to play.

Coach Winett was in no hurry to start Rod. The small senior had to work for everything he would get and prove that he was the best guy for his position—free safety. The basic thing Rod learned about the playing part of it was to line up on the two-receiver side of the field, about twelve yards deep, and never let anyone get behind him. The rest of the defensive game for him was reading plays, and going to the ball.

Rod was smart so he was a quick study when watching any quarterback. He was fearless so nothing and no one intimidated him. And, he was fast with great balance. But there was the matter of Rod's temper and his need to be larger than he was.

On one of those afternoons when Rod was showing attitude Coach Winett took him aside. "You can take a lesson from all of this, or you can fold." Rod listened and took the advice to heart.

At the season's end the stats told the story. Grant Union was tied for first place in their district that consisted of eight schools of the Greater Oregon League. They had six wins and three losses overall, with five wins and two losses in league play. The league team they tied with for first, Vale High School, went to the state playoffs only because they had recorded a victory over Grant Union during the regular season.

For Rod it proved to be a great year. Of thirty-six possible quarters of play he had played in twenty-seven. A thigh injury kept him out of a few quarters. His stats included: thirty-two assisted tackles; eleven unassisted tackles; and four interceptions, of which two were in one game. That last accomplishment put him in a first place tie for the Grant Union All-Time record of interceptions in one game. To the pride of his school, his family, and himself, he received an "Honorable Mention" as free safety for the Greater Oregon League in 1976.

For Gene Winett that season was a springboard for Rod. He had seen the young man's desire drive him past others on the field. Rod was always competitive, took coaching well though a bit surly at times. The coach knew that Rod, like all young men, needed to mature. If he survived growing up he had potential to do something great.

As a great indicator to Gene, at the season's end Rod walked up to him and said, "Coach, I'm really glad I had a chance to work with you. Thanks. I learned a lot."

During those years at Grant Union there were not many who could effectively tease Rod about his size. One exception to that limitation was L.J. "Pete" Baucum. While he taught biology, Pete loved rodeo. He had been teaching at Grant Union long enough to experience and really appreciated both Rick and Rod. Pete had managed kid's rodeo during the 1950s and 1960s. He knew well about the young ones trying to emulate the cowboys.

In school, every now and again, he would catch a young teen taking their first chew. He made a few chew up that Beechnut and then swallow. As they would run for the bathroom Pete knew he had cured another one, for a while at least. It was a sad day when Pete learned about Rick's death the year before. School was out but everyone in town heard the news within hours.

In school Pete kept things normal and wanted Rod to participate. At the beginning of the fall semester he asked the class about their respective summers. When it came around to Rod, Pete kept it light.

"Rod, how was rodeo for you this summer?" He already knew that Rod had a couple of wins.

"Won me a bull ride or two," Rod responded.

"Well, its good you figured out that your legs aren't long enough to get them bucking horses started out of the chute." Pete had a way of delivering such barbs so that they would land easily. Rod would take the opportunity to tease back, and some of his words were self-effacing. Other times he would enhance the joke since he trusted Pete and he knew that some of what he did was pretty darn humorous. That reciprocal trust comes from mutual respect. The next year it was the same Pete who took a lot of pride in announcing that Rod had qualified for the bareback riding competition at the high school nationals taking place in Sulfa, Louisiana.

In addition to biology and loving rodeo Pete also taught classes that fell under the general heading of conservation. A part of that learning was firearm safety. Rifles and guns were as commonplace as cell phones are in the 21st Century. Looking out to the parking lot anyone would see that virtually every pickup truck had at least one loaded rifle hanging behind the driver's head. The doors were never locked. No one thought one way or the other about it. This was simply a part of rural farm and ranch life. Kids learned what weapons were about and what to use them for from a very early age.

Rod wanted to keep up the athletic effort after his senior

football season. His choice was track and field. His freshman year he had joined the track team, again being coached by Morgan Groath. It was a good experience and it filled that need Rod had for challenging himself. His improvements were immediately accessible through the recorded times or the jump distances.

An Italian Portuguese red headed fellow named Chuck Toste was the new track coach. Rod liked the directness of this twenty-six year old immediately. Toste established a no-nonsense policy day one. He would give out demerits in P.E. that lowered the student's grade, unless the student elected to come in early and work the demerit off.

The work Toste had in mind that could remove a demerit was running a mile in under seven minutes. Accomplish that and one demerit would be removed. For a variety of reasons Rod got a lot of demerits and therefore gladly put in his early morning time removing them. The trouble Rod would find himself in often resulted from using his mouth to insure that he was being respected, since in his mind few in class took him seriously.

Coach Toste had played football at Eastern Washington State College and the Grant Union High School job was his first teaching assignment. Rod saw him as someone who was bringing real experience to the school. Also, in Rod's view it was evident that the coach treated him as an equal to all the other team members.

Rod's senior year accomplishments in track were those of a much taller boy. At only five feet four inches he took his four years of practicing the high hurdles, his concentration on each stride, his reaching and stretching of his legs, and kept his aim on making it to the district track meet.

His best time previously had been 16.8 and he was expected to place about seventh based on all the times of the competitors. To

Rod's advantage on that day was all the bull riding he had been doing. One would not necessarily think of riding one-ton bulls as training for the high hurdles, but in this case, stretching out for those bulls and the broncs gave him a big advantage. He could do the splits anyway he wanted to. Rod had learned to be totally flexible and agile or those big bulls would tear up his groin.

At the district meet Rod ran his best race ever. His normal experience would only allow him to three-step the first four hurdles. Then he would hit the rest of the hurdles with alternate legs, and that would slow him down. The taller boys could three-step them all.

That beautiful day at the district meet Rod owned the track. The feeling was deep in his gut. In the hurdles he got out fast and hit the first one perfectly. He managed to three-step all the hurdles but the last one, barely hitting it with his trailing leg.

Coach Toste and the rest of Rod's team could not help but notice that people in the stands were paying a lot of attention to this little guy from John Day. The other team's fans and some of the coaches were cheering Rod on. That last hurdle did allow Rod's teammate, who was the top seed, to edge him out for first at the tape. But Rod Retherford ran a 15.8, one full second better than his best time. He finished second overall and shocked coach Toste by qualifying for the state games.

At five-feet four inches, even though he ran a 15.3 at state, Rod was eliminated in the first round. But he was thrilled to be a part of that event. His team was proud of him too. In the spirit of the whole thing they threw Rod in the pool after the first day to celebrate his being knocked out in the first round. It was all in great fun and Rod loved every second of it.

Chuck Toste had his biggest impact on Rod though, off the track. And on the way to a track meet, with Rod riding in the coach's car, another side of Rod was witnessed. Chuck had made a mistake in traffic that angered another driver. Being a really responsible guy Chuck stopped to apologize. The driver was blowing off steam, not wanting to accept the goodwill of the apology and began to argue with Chuck. Rod, almost a foot shorter than the driver, came out of the car and stepped up alongside his coach quite ready to get physical.

"Need any help here, coach?" he asked, looking up the driver with an intimidating glare.

"No thanks, Rod. I think the gentleman is accepting my apology."

After a moment the driver realized he was making a mistake and gave up the argument. In that same moment Chuck Toste understood that Rod would take anything or anybody on, if it meant helping a friend.

Later Chuck would tell Rod, "Get out of John Day. There's a whole world out there waiting for you." He said it several times and one day those words became part of what led Rod to follow his dream. Had Coach Jones not been at the pool that summer day, if he had assumed that since Rod did not play football his junior year it was because he did not want to, or if Coach Toste had not shared his eagerness to have students spread their wings, Rod Retherford might have spent his life as a pond monkey.

In the years that followed Chuck Toste raised his own family, and became the proud father of a son, Travis, who grew to six feet two inches and became quite an athlete. Chuck would grab the yearbook from his first days at Grant Union and point to a picture of little Rod Retherford.

"See this little kid, Travis. At five feet four inches he could run faster than you."

In the day when Rod was a senior, little could he have realized that he would inspire the kids who come to that school and others, well after his days there. However, what he faced now that he was home from Pullman was a greater challenge than his size had ever been.

10.

Those first four weeks back in John Day after dropping out of Washington State University were lost to a continuation of the depression that set in the first week of the fall semester. The number of pain pills Rod needed also served to dim the reality of his life. His days were on the couch, nights in bed, and the farthest he would walk was to the bathroom.

Sleep was interrupted by the continued sound of the pistol firing. He would wake from deep sleep to that frightening memory of the bullet hitting him, his one arm flailing in a hopeless attempt to deflect the experience. Soaked in sweat from the deep stress that would precede the awakening sound, Rod would find no relief. This was a nightmare that continued to live with him. He was also dropping weight fast. In those four weeks he lost thirty-five pounds.

During the daylight hours, drifting in and out of consciousness, he would find himself back in better times when the future promised him everything and his mortality was never a thought. On the other hand the emotional swing would take him to the question of how much of life was left ahead of him?

Those stones stepped past, that instead might have been turned over to reveal the gold, those pretty girls he might have kissed but never had the chance to because being small was not desirable, the football games he would have played, but now with a dead arm who would want him? Certainly not Stacey!

Her wonderful face and that long hair had popped up in Rod's thoughts as if their September 1976 meeting at the *Pendleton Round Up* was last week. Rod was at Pendleton with Calvin Clark. This was a big year for the Round Up because the Hall of Fame room under the south grandstand had been completed and was in use. It also marked the first event since the *Pendleton Round Up* had agreed to the PRCA's negotiating demand over five months, to a thirty percent increase in the purse.

The world famous Round Up had almost reached its seventieth birthday, it having found its beginning following a July 4th celebration in 1909. That first year bronc riding, horse races by Indians and whites, Indian feasts and war dances, greased pig contests, sack races, foot races and fireworks, gave birth to the annual event.

Fresh from his senior year of high school and his football and track accomplishments, a good summer of rodeo, and starting to sprout, Rod was feeling pretty cocky. He and Calvin had gone to the big dance being held at the Armory on the first night of the Round Up. That's when he first saw Stacey Snow. She was five feet five inches tall, her brunette hair straight and pulled back into a single ponytail that passed her waist, a smile that stopped Rod in his tracks. She was a heart-stopper of a country girl.

Rod's confidence was high from all his accomplishments of the year, so he asked Stacey to dance. She agreed and they took to the floor while the Leroy Van Dyke band was performing. His famous tune *Auctioneer* had sold three million copies by that time. This dance was a big event by any standard and it was to become a landmark in Rod's life.

Moving across the floor Rod took a hold of Stacey's hand and knew immediately he should not let go of her. Yes, she was young, about fourteen. Rod was seventeen. Seeing themselves together they looked just right since he was small for his age and young looking, and Stacey was fairly tall. Rod was a gentleman cowboy, despite being a cocky young buck. His cowboy quality resonated with Stacey since her dad was just that.

For Rod, lying on the living room couch with depression transfixing his mind, thoughts of Stacey from four years earlier were powerful. He remembered how electric he felt while holding her hand. He had never felt a power like that. This was love, though he had no way to realize it then. This was not some drive-in movie score. In many sport related experiences Rod had felt power in the physical sense, but the power this beautiful lithe young woman had with him was completely new and she practically took his legs out from under him.

Calvin had hooked up with a girl and was happy to be on his own. He and Rod had driven to Pendleton in Jim Retherford's Ford pickup and Rod had the keys. Stacey had come to the dance from her home in Echo, Oregon accompanied by her older sister, Lisa. Echo was about thirty miles from Pendleton.

As the evening progressed Rod was convinced that he should not let the night separate him from Stacey. In his favor was his friendship with young Zane Gibbs who was the son of a stock contractor that Rod knew well from rodeo. Zane was dating Lisa and when Rod suggested that he could drive Stacey home, everyone was fine with the idea.

During these hours with Stacey, Rod had been struck by Cupid's arrow for the first time in his young life. As he guided Stacey to the pickup truck, parked some hundred yards down the road in a quiet spot, he had this overwhelming feeling that there was nothing else in the world that mattered. On the other hand Stacey was too inexperienced with life to realize what she might have been feeling, the depth to which those feelings were rooted.

The truck was two-tone white with orange panels. It had a white canopy over the truck bed, and in the customary fashion of a "Cowboy Motel," there was a mattress under the canopy. The two teens climbed onto the truck bed and curled up. As much as Rod wanted to fulfill his body's burning desires he stayed true to form and was a gentleman. They necked, he was tender and caressing with her, but never crossed the line from innocence. At about 3:30 that morning he drove Stacey home, hating the approaching sunrise.

Stacey slipped into her family's ranch house without waking anyone. Later that morning, after asking her mother, she invited Rod to come in for breakfast. That innocent evening would never leave Rod's memory. Young love has a way of staying with us our entire lives. But, in this case there was another reason for the memory staying alive, and Rod was yet to discover this.

Chris was a serious basketball player and Rod being back in the house during his recovery meant once again sharing the small bedroom. In earlier years all three brothers bunked together using a combination of a military style bunk bed and a single for Rick.

One of the lost afternoons of that first four weeks, Chris was home from practice early and sat with Rod in the living room. He could see that his big brother was in pain, and even though he wanted to help he had no idea what to do. He decided to talk, to express to Rod what he had bottled up.

"When I heard you were shot I just couldn't believe that God would let you die. And you didn't."

"Yeah, and here I am, me and my bum arm," Rod replied with an obvious degree of sarcasm.

"Better than what almost happened."

"It shouldn't have happened at all."

"But it did. And you're home." Chris felt for Rod but would not let him be negative.

Rod had nothing more to say so it was quiet for a bit, just the television chatter of "Hollywood Squares" in the background.

Chris began to reflect. "We used to have some great dirt-clod fights."

That brought a very small grin to Rod's face. "Yeah, I remember them days. I especially remember how pissed mom got at me when she had dressed you for Easter dinner over at the Elliotts. You were all shiny and scrubbed wearing a nice white shirt when you walked out front to remind me to get ready. Next thing mom saw was you and I in a dirt-clod fight."

The boys laughed a little over the funny part of that story.

Then Chris took a deeper turn. "Don't think I ever told you this—the year after Rick died, that entire school year, I would bust out of class and run for my bike. I would peddle home as fast as I could, and run in the front door."

"Why?" Rod asked sincerely.

"I was certain that if I sped home, when I came through the

front door Rick would be sitting at the kitchen table talking to mom."

"Wow. Chris, what a bummer."

"Everyday. I was such a little kid at ten. I was so excited. It's like believing in Santa Claus. I just knew he would be there. Every afternoon after the dream would get busted I would slide into a funk."

"It's a wonder any of us got through it," Rod added.

"Yeah. Sure is." Chris got up and walked towards the kitchen. "You want anything?"

"Nope."

Chris returned with a glass of milk and sat down. "Especially dad. Can't say how many times I opened the door and found him passed out in the afternoon. Depression! Mom and him, they did the best they knew how for me. Mom, she tried hard to keep everything like normal. But alls I remember is her getting up from the kitchen table crying. You ask me about dinners at that time and that's what I remember."

"It was horrible. To dad, if we had gone to get help from a counselor, we'd been sissies," Rod added. "But I know they did what they knew how to do. I mean where do you learn how to deal with the death of a son?"

Chris finished his glass of milk. "It was like living in Fantasyland. Our brother died. We went to the funeral. We buried him up on top of the hill. But nobody would talk about it at home. I had the feeling all those years that everyone thought I was too young to understand."

"Hey, you were only ten," Rod added.

"I still felt the pain of his death. And I missed my big brother. He can't come back. I stopped that silly kid thing after the first year."

"It wasn't silly Chris. It was a good thing to hope like that. Probably helped you get through those days."

Chris turned the tables on Rod. "I'll tell you what a good thing is, Rod. You ain't parked up on that hill in the space next to Rick. You're sitting right here and we're having a conversation the way it was meant to be."

Chris just looked at his big brother. Again there was silence. Chris had just popped Rod between the eyes with powerful childhood experiences that gave the older brother pause. Suddenly there was more to this than what Rod himself was experiencing emotionally. Chris inadvertently had found a key that would help Rod unravel the emotional barrier that his depression had seized.

After Rick's death Rod was numb. He wanted to cry but never had. What Chris said to him a few hours earlier had taken Rod to that time of mourning. He kept imagining his little ten-year-old brother's legs pushing as hard as they could every afternoon, pumping on those bike pedals to make the impossible happen. Innocent hope and dreams, the desire to make things right, to somehow correct a terrible wrong—in the ten-year-old mind that was possible. On the day that Chris gave that dream up, he gave up his childhood. This brought tears to Rod's eyes.

Mitch Gregg's dad, Gary, had a profound effect on Rod four weeks after Rick's accident. Rod had stopped riding rodeo. Not from any fear, quite the contrary. He loathed the accident that took his brother. His anger clouded his thoughts and virtually Rod's life was on hold.

Gary hated to see Rod in this turmoil and knew that the young man needed to bust himself loose from the proverbial holding pen he was constricted by, much like the bull waiting to toss the rider on its back. He posed a simple blunt question to Rod.

"If Rick had been driving a car and an auto accident took his life, would you have stopped driving?"

Rod was a little confounded by the simplicity of the question. The answer was obvious.

Gary continued with, "So why would you walk away from something that Rick loved and that you love, and that you are damn good at? Do you really think Rick would want you to swear off Rodeo?"

The initial comparative quality of the question, giving up driving because someone died driving, was still ringing in Rod's ears. This question led him right back to rodeo competition and a win on the first bull he rode. And here, four years later, Rick's sudden death was again serving Rod in his current state of life.

In the dark of that night Rod drove himself up the road from town to the cemetery. He made the left turn from the country road and rolled onto that mountaintop. The night was clear and cold. He headed down the center lane of the cemetery and then turned right, parking the car in front of Rick's tombstone. Rod started playing a cassette of Eric Clapton's version of "Knockin' On Heaven's Door," left the car door open so the music would fill the cemetery, and sat down, his back leaning against Rick's tombstone.

Of the many images that raced through his consciousness, one was striking him now. On the day of Rick's memorial, when Rod walked to the open casket to have the final view of his big brother, he was struck by the impulse to give Rick the championship calf riding buckle he was wearing. So as he stood at the casket Rod removed his buckle and belt, coiled it, and then placed it with his brother. Several of Rod's friends saw this gesture. Some of those friends were also wearing trophy buckles that Rod had loaned them, and taking his lead, they too removed the buckles and placed them in the casket. Rick had been a champion to many, especially his brothers, and it gave Rod great comfort to know that Rick would have this physical evidence with him for eternity.

This day, passing into memory and joining so much of Rod's experiences, was in a manner of speaking a day of reckoning. There was no one Rod would rather discuss the dilemmas with, or rejoice with, than Rick. The veil of night surrounding Rick's eternal hilltop home was the place for such communion.

The next morning Rod got out of bed with a plan. He felt a new wave of determination and purpose, and this was a new day. There was a way for him to achieve his dream and all that was preventing it to this point was Rod Retherford.

11.

Rod's right hand was working, but the shoulder muscles had begun to atrophy to such an extent that his scapula, shoulder blade, was protruding from his back. If his right arm were raised up by another person and let go of, it would drop to his leg. He had no control and considered himself dead on the right side.

Doctors had discussed all of this with Rod and explained that the anterior, front side, of the scapula reveals the subscapular fossa to which the subscapularis muscle attaches. The subscapularis is a large triangular muscle. The Latin words were off-putting, but the physical function served was what Rod needed to understand. He learned that the subscapularis rotates the head of the humerus, the long bone in the arm that runs from the shoulder to the elbow. The doctors had further explained that the scapula also articulates with the clavicle. But Rod realized that his subscapularis was a non-starter, probably the result of the bullet passing through it. Preparing himself for what might be the eventual outcome— having a dead arm—could be a fact of his life.

Waking that morning after his conversation with Chris, Rod sat up and said to himself, "Life is too short for B.S. It's on the wire everyday, and the rest is just waiting." He walked to the bathroom and stood at the mirror.

There he asked himself a question. "What can a one-armed football player do effectively?"

"Kick!" he answered with authority. "That will put me back with the Cougs." Then he blurted out, "You better get yer ass in gear, Retherford."

Rod needed to develop the skill on his own so he would become a place-kicker for the Cougars. Why not? The position had become specialized in the '60s and Rod knew he could fill it. Until the 1960s the kicker was almost always doubled at another position on the team roster, George Blanda having been a great example, being a kicker and quarterback.

Rod had always done well in the Punt, Pass & Kick competition during his school days so he knew he was pretty accurate. He also knew he could crank out the distance.

Rod first knew he had the kicking potential during the days of Little League Football. Jim entered the youngster in the Punt, Pass & Kick. A fellow named Paul Smith won, Rod placed second, Tom Dieker placed third. Only thing was that Rod did not have football shoes like the other boys. He came out their wearing his boots.

When the scoring was announced one of the other competitor's father was practically apoplectic. He demanded that Rod be disqualified because those boots must have given the boy an advantage, or so the dad argued.

Rod did not care, but Jim was not going to let this disagreement ruin his son's day. He argued with the judges and the result was the opportunity of a re-kick, with Rod wearing acceptable footwear.

Since Rod had no football shoes Jim took him home and got the one pair of leather oxfords his son would wear for school. Rod was embarrassed by the whole ordeal but did as his dad wanted. They returned to the field. The judges okayed the oxfords. The complaining dad had no issue with them either.

So Rod re-kicked. This time to everyone's shock, Rod's kick was the most accurate and the longest. He defeated Paul Smith who moved to the number two spot. Tom Dieker remained in third. The father who complained had nothing more to say.

When they presented the trophy to Rod he did not want to accept it. As far as he was concerned Paul had won the competition fair and square the first time through. Be that as it may, Rod knew from that day on that he had kicking skills. His competition kicks were always within three feet of the tape on either side.

Rod searched through the boy's room closet that fall morning of his revelation. He found four footballs. After some breakfast he put those footballs in a plastic trash bag and drove over to the high school. Since classes were in session he had the football field to himself. He set up a tee and began practicing his kicking.

The first few weeks he would limp back to his car because he was pushing himself hard on the field. Those never-been used muscles needed to develop. However, he firmly believed that with his heart and love of the sport, and with the time he would invest, he would make this happen.

Soon Rod could tell that the minimum four hours a day were paying off. After eight weeks of kicking Rod was very consistent from forty yards out. During all this development he had begun to experiment with soccer-style kicks. He went from a straight-on kicker to soccer-style and gained distance. It worked so well he got to the point where he could cut them in from sixty yards out.

It was a great relief to the family that Rod had raised himself off the couch and begun to compete for a life. The darkness that came with the depression was gone. During those eight weeks he was kicking, a few of Rod's school friends ran into him. One of those was Kelly Lemons with whom he had played Little League. Kelly had seen Rod's development post high school and was very aware of his weight training accomplishment with Max Hull prior to his walk-on to WSU. Kelly also knew Chris well through their interest in basketball.

One afternoon, seeing Rod walking to his car from the football field and kicking practice, Kelly stopped to talk to his old friend. After the pleasantries he got to a very important point.

"You have always been an inspiration around these parts, Rod. You believed in yourself when no one else seemed to, when nobody wanted to give you a chance," Kelly said.

Rod had not expected to hear this and it caught him off guard. He could not respond before Kelly continued.

"I saw you get bucked off bulls and get right back on. We're talkin' two thousand pounds of snorting angry bull that would just as soon kill you as do anything. So tell me, what's a bullet? It didn't kill you—so I know you'll play football again."

Rod drove home that afternoon thankful to have heard those words from Kelly. To know that people in the town, his school peers, were aware of what his school years had been. This all was an amazing acknowledgement.

As younger people are wont to do when they suddenly feel a need to make life-altering change, they will jump to what is imagined might be a better way of living—the "assumed adult, acting like a grownup" behavior. Rod was no exception to this phenomenon. Having dated Patti earlier in the summer, having been intimate with her then, having her show interest in being with him after his injury, and being that she had moved back to John Day from DuBois, Idaho, when he dropped out of school, Rod began seeing Patti daily.

She had real nurturing and motherly tendencies and, in his weakened condition, Rod was ripe for such attention and affection. One of the thoughts that plagued him, since mortality kept surfacing through those horrible nightmares of the gun shot and during the days as he worked to overcome his physical limitation, was the knowledge that a person might be here in one instance and gone from the earth in another. Who knew how much time might be given to their mortal life? So Rod was beginning to think about getting busy with the next phase of life: marriage and having a family.

Patti made it very clear that she wanted children. She had a background in sports through volleyball, basketball, and track. They came from the same valley, had a lot of friends in common, and all of it seemed comfortable. But then what can anyone know of adult life when barely twenty-one years old? And how would Rod know what world was left out there for him to conquer?

So Patti and Rod became very involved while he worked to prepare himself to re-enter the football program at Washington State University. He knew there was no guarantee with any of his plan. In the cold light of day, stepping aside from his enthusiasm, he realized that he might not find himself the best choice as the WSU place-kicker. Then he would face the question of school— to finish getting his four-year degree or enter the work force to finance his life. As much as he considered alternatives one thing that was certain, if he did not act on his impulses now, he realized that something lurking around the next corner of the road of life might bring his life to a sudden close.

His thoughts would continually return to a question that plagues many when they begin a search for the meaning of their life. If Rod died what would there be of Rod Retherford that anyone would remember, that would have given purpose to his being here? A child of his own, he thought. The continuation of a legacy was within his grasp.

12.

Not too far from the Retherford home in 1974 sat the Grant County Fair Grounds in John Day. It had covered stadium seating that sat seven hundred fifty people as a part of the park facilities. It was the fitting location for Rick's memorial and virtually everyone in town was there.

The news of Rick's death had muted the town. Along the main drag the austere silence was evident in every doorway, sales counter, restaurant, sidewalk, and crosswalk. Folks were passing without making eye contact. What could anyone say? He was as well known as anyone in town. Rick Retherford was a bright light whose glow of humanity was a constant blessing. On that day the collective spirit of the town was kicked in its solar plexus. The gasping for some breathable understanding would only be satisfied after many months passed, disconnecting the very present from what would become the distant.

James Retherford, though a totally distraught father, spoke

at his boy's memorial service. Milo Frankie, the minister at the Assembly of God Church and longtime friend of the family, delivered the service that July day. Rod, Mitch, and another musician friend, Greg Wygant performed "Knockin' On Heaven's Door". Later, Rod could not remember much more than a blur of faces, everyone that ever knew Rick.

In the winter of 1981 as Rod diligently practiced place-kicking daily, he would pass these grounds. He had chosen not to talk about what he was doing for fear that people would laugh at him. His dad had been through something quite similar, people laughing at an overt change in the man, and Rod was gaining a greater understanding of Jim in these days of physical challenge.

Rod was channeling his determination to overcome his physical limitation, using that stimulus as a powerful antidote to the otherwise life threatening toxins of depression.

His dad had survived the same dynamic. However, the catalyst for healing in Jim's instance was ultimately given him by his father—that day nearly a year prior the senior James' last breath when, after a lifetime of cursing and lack of interest in religion, he acknowledged the existence of a higher power. Rod knew the steps from his grandfather's acknowledgement of God took his dad on a road embraced by Betty. Jim opened himself to spiritual awareness, to enlightenment, to a realization that there was a power far greater than what any mortal might possess.

But there was a price, one of humility that came with this newly and openly professed belief. When Jim Retherford announced his intention to study for the ministry of the Assembly of God Church under the tutelage of Milo Frankie, the cynics in the community laughed.

"How could this man suddenly preach the bible?" was asked in gossipy circles of criticism.

Rod could not help but think about his dad's transformation and the ridicule he had faced. While Rod wanted to protect himself from the same, just leave town one morning having mastered place-kicking, arrive at Pullman, walk-on and make the team, he understood that the world has plenty of doubters. It is a safer place for many to be on the negative side, to question change, to not believe. But, Rod was blessed with a positive way of approaching life and he was keeping himself focused on just that.

During Rod's quest for a new position in his football career, and while he had suffered such weight loss during the immediate weeks after suffering the gunshot, he needed to put back some of the weight he had dropped. This was an imperative or he would never be seen as a serious candidate by WSU. His mom was glad to see him begin eating as much as she could put in front of him. At the same time Rod returned to the free weights to build muscle mass. This proved to be another major challenge.

Not having a right arm made bench work impossible. He was faced with developing one side of his body and that would only make matters worse. It was another friend who entered at that moment and helped Rod recover.

Brad Krayer had played high school football with Rod. This school friend paid Rod a visit one afternoon. As the two spoke about their recent years Rod was to learn that Brad's girlfriend, Cindy White, had suffered major injuries from an automobile accident. She was a quadriplegic. Brad had been taught by hospital therapists and had done his own studies about what he could do to help her with daily exercises of her otherwise motionless limbs. He had a natural understanding of the dynamic, was a very giving kind of young man, and therefore had much experience now.

Brad offered to help Rod with resistance training. He had done a lot of research while helping Cindy, always hoping for the miracle but also knowing how critical it was for her wellbeing that this effort be applied daily.

Resistance training has two different, sometimes confused meanings—a more broad meaning that refers to any training that uses a resistance to the force of muscular contraction. This is better termed strength training. Elastic or hydraulic resistance, which refers to a specific type of strength training that uses elastic or hydraulic tension to provide this resistance, is the other.

Each effort in this form of training is performed against a specific opposing force generated by resistance: resistance to being pushed, squeezed, stretched or bent as typical examples. Exercises are isotonic if a body part is moving against the force. Exercises are isometric if a body part is holding still against the force. Resistance exercise is used to develop the strength and size of skeletal muscles. Properly performed, resistance training can provide significant functional benefits and improvement in overall health and well-being.

According to the American Sports Medicine Institute the goal of resistance training is to "gradually and progressively overload the musculoskeletal system so it gets stronger." Research shows that regular resistance training will strengthen and tone muscles and increase bone mass.

Rod knew well about plyometrics through weightlifting, power-lifting and bodybuilding. He also knew about immovable resistance and isometrics, usually the body's own muscles or a structural feature such as a doorframe or the floor being used in exercises like pushups.

Rod gladly accepted the offer, so Brad began working with

him. Brad certainly had no way of knowing whether Rod's right shoulder would ever come back to life giving him use of his right arm. He offered no false promise. As far as Brad was concerned they were just a couple of guys trying to make things right.

Each day Brad worked with him he would take Rod's right arm, extend it while supporting the elbow joint, have Rod make a fist in the palm of Brad's hand, and then have him try to resist Brad pushing towards him. This became a ritual. Week after week the same routine was applied, and always the same result was reached. Rod had no resistance he could offer with his right arm.

During this time Rod shared his kicking ambition with Brad.

Brad responded to the idea positively. "You know Rod, I think you are a great athlete. You were as a kid, you obviously were one before the accident, and you still are. You have the desire and the fortitude. If you have your mind set on kicking then I guess that's what you will achieve."

Rod appreciated the encouragement. "You know, bud, I kicked a sixty yarder yesterday. I am getting real consistent from closer in. This ain't so much a dream anymore. I know I can be a kicker. And, if that's it, if that's the position I can play, then I'll earn it!"

"I'm sure," Brad said. A couple moments of thought were followed with, "But, don't let your mind give up on what we're doing here. Who knows, maybe one day you'll at least be able to raise that arm."

And so these two friends who grew up in the same little town in the Pacific Northwest, who went to the same schools, who competed with each other in the same sports, who had gone down different roads after high school, were coming together with a common goal. There were no hi-tech therapy machines, clinics, medical plans or doctors. It was the sheer will of two guys at work here.

For Brad this was an altruistic gesture, a window looking into his belief in a friend. It was also revealing of his desire to give something of himself to the ones who needed him. For Rod it was further acknowledgement of his athletic destiny, and more importantly, a statement from his peers, the ones he had heard giggle when he was handed shoulder pads that didn't fit, the ones who laughed with Pete and Rod when the joke about his legs being too short for horses was made; to now have these same kids as adults, step up and come to Rod's side, it brought a meaning to life that had never existed for him till this moment.

The world of the Cougars of Washington State University was there for Rod. All he had to do was get back to Pullman, he thought. But his body had another surprise waiting for him that would change this plan. As Rod would come to learn again and again, we may have our plans, but the Big Guy above has the ability to overrule us at any moment.

13.

Once Rod made the decision to get off the couch and start training so he would have a reasonable chance to re-enter the Cougar football program, everything in his life was brighter. The daily kicking practice, the workout regimen, the conscious planning of the steps he needed to take to meet his goal, the mental checklist he religiously covered daily, and the acts of support and belief from his family, from friends like Brad, the accumulation of all this added up to confidence. Even though Rod was a "can do" kind of guy, having emotional support was the basis of this powerful drive that he now tapped into.

Betty and Jim were at the forefront of his column of believers. Since Jim's return from Oklahoma he had begun his studies for the ministry, a change that Rod and Chris struggled to accept. They saw the transformation, the change in behavior, the lifting from the grip of depression, the elimination of foul language from his daily routine, but they were waiting for the return of all those negative traits they had spent their lives with.

On a quiet evening Betty sat down on the couch with Rod to have her after dinner coffee. Rod knew there was more than a chat in this gesture when she put her hand on his, and said, "Rod, we are so thankful that you have recovered. Your dad and I thank the Lord every minute of the day for the miracle."

"I'm getting there, Mom, day by day."

She continued. "And everyday as I see you go off to practice, watch how dedicated you are, and see your determination continue to push you, well I believe all our prayers are being answered."

She shifted her position turning more towards him. There was a pensive quality to her face. This was rapidly developing into an emotional moment and he did not know if his mom was about to cry, so his instinct was to comfort her. He patted her on the hand and she gave him one of those motherly smiles of hers. He had carried many of those with him since he was a little kid. The mere flash of her smile of understanding brought him comfort during many moments of extreme challenge.

Betty had more she needed to say. She prepared to launch on her real mission of the moment. "Since you went off to Treasure Valley College I've not seen you show any interest in going to church. I think, no, I know its time for you to take up an earnest effort for a spiritual path in your life. As much as you work at building physical skill, work at disciplining yourself with the routine you follow so well, you need to apply to God and ask for guidance."

Betty was studying his face, trying to read his expression to learn whether he was really understanding how a spiritual pursuit was critical for him in this moment. Whether he was ready to open his mind or not, she was determined to not only voice her concern, but to make a demand on him. More than anything, Betty wanted to hasten the arrival of that day when Rod accomplished his ambitious goal—the day when Rod no longer felt he had to overcome being too short or small. He had survived the years of ridicule when he was the littlest in class, the devastating pain after Rick's death, his own brush with death, so now it was time for Rod to have his dreams come true. Betty was convinced that spiritual development would unlock the doorway he needed to step through. In this moment she was certainly voicing thoughts she had discussed with Jim, however, this was the mother speaking to the child. This was Betty answering to her responsibility as a parent, addressing her purpose in being here.

Rod responded very directly. "Okay, Mom. That sounds like something I should do." His smile projected an absolute acceptance of her request.

"Good. We'll go to church together on Sunday."

"That's what we'll do," he said with a positive tone.

He knew he had just given his mom a great gift, a sense of peace and relief of concern. That knowledge made Rod feel complete for this day. She had gone to the kitchen to finish her day's work, and even though Rod seemed zoned out on the television, he was reeling back through her words and his response.

Rod was not placating Betty with his immediate agreement. Everything she stated was to the point. All the time that Rod had mourned Rick's death he had pursued a path that was very destructive. It was a miracle, possibly of Rick's making, that Rod had come through those dark days. All the time Rod spent in conversation with Rick up at his gravesite was much like prayer. Rod was discussing life with his brother. But his brother was now part of the heavens and so in a way, Rod had already begun praying. The only difference now, he would say his prayers in church.

Rod's workouts with Brad were on an aggressive schedule.

Brad never asked the question, "Why didn't you have physical therapy prescribed at the hospital?"

Brad knew the answer. If Rod could have afforded the kind of therapy provided by hospitals with injury cases such as his he would have had a rehabilitation team working with him to improve his remaining muscle strength and to give him the greatest possible mobility and independence.

Rod's team might have included a physical therapist, occupational therapist, rehabilitation nurse, rehabilitation psychologist, social worker, dietitian recreation therapist and a doctor who specializes in physical medicine, a physiatrist, or spinal cord injury specialist.

During the initial stages of rehabilitation, therapists would have emphasized regaining leg and arm strength, redeveloping fine-motor skills and learning adaptive techniques to accomplish day-to-day tasks. They would have followed guidelines developed over time from studies of thousands of medical cases.

Rod's therapy would have begun in the Spokane hospital and continued in a rehabilitation facility there. As his therapy continued, Rod and his family would have received counseling and assistance on a wide range of topics.

Rod would also have had the benefit of medications that manage the signs, symptoms and complications of spinal cord injury. Those would have included medications to control pain and muscle spasticity.

Inventive medical devices such as electrical stimulation devices and neural prostheses might have been employed to further rehabilitate Rod. These sophisticated devices would have used electrical stimulation to produce actions. They might have implanted some under the skin and connected them with the nervous system to supplement or replace lost motor and sensory functions. Others might have been used outside the body, electrical stimulators to control arm and leg muscles to allow people with a spinal cord injury to stand, walk, reach and grip.

With all of the typical procedures for physical therapy stated, all those remarkable methods available to those who have the insurance policy, or the financial capability of underwriting such treatment, would have been expected for Rod.

However, in Rod Retherford's case, none of this was available. Rod was sent home from the hospital in Spokane with drugs to relieve his pain and what amounted to a band-aid over each bullet hole. He had no insurance policy. His family did not have the kind of money necessary to finance such professional treatment. This type of care would have consumed tens of thousands of dollars. Plus, Rod had showed such an amazingly quick recovery in the first hours, and he was able to walk, that he was sent back to the world from which he came.

Relying on himself, not depending on others to make things happen, was something Rod had long ago learned. Brad was an exception because Rod needed someone to work with him, and Rod knew that Brad had firsthand experience with this. What Rod had not expected was Brad's determination to have his friend recover some use of his right arm was as great as Rod's desire.

Rod was quite used to seeing results from training. The work with Brad was a new experience. When the right arm showed no signs of strengthening, Brad was not phased. At times during his workouts with Brad, Rod would find his thoughts wandering. The two friends would be progressing through the regimen of resistance training that Brad believed in, but while this was going on he would notice that Rod's attention would drift. Brad knew that Rod was in a transitional stage and that a part of that evolution was mental and emotional.

Surviving a microscopically close brush with death should bring change to the survivor's approach to life. In the practical mind one would, at minimum, expect some serious contemplation. Yes, Rod knew how death could snatch someone right before his eyes. He once again took eight seconds of his life and thought through each click. Rick had been just across the arena in plain sight at second one on the clock. He was riding with all the skill and energy a seventeen-year-old could have, however by second eight on that same clock Rick was gone from the earth.

Those eight seconds had become hours and days and months. The experience was an octagonal progression, a time sequence that resolved itself in such torment as to give Rod a practical theory that he would apply to the balance of his life. The core of the theory was formed out of regret. Rod and Rick, as all Homo sapiens do, argued. Rod certainly knew disagreement between brothers so closely involved was natural. Different minds will have their singular perspective on any site, subject, or sound. He also understood that holding apart from betrayal of fundamental trust, disagreements in familial or romantic relationships that carry on beyond the moment they were expressed were all too common. A minute, an hour, a day later, the participants in the emotional dance of discord usually found their way past the conflict—unless eight seconds of destiny seized the life from one of the players.

The continued absurdity in all of Rod's thoughts—he could not remember why it was that he was mad at Rick on that June day. Eight seconds and whatever caused Rod to walk to the other side of the arena was gone. This now propelled Rod to seize each second of his life and not let the proverbial grass grow under his feet while something of no lasting meaning ground momentum to a halt. Factoring into this aggressive attitude—the comprehension that a hair's movement in either his own movements or the direction of Junior Tupuola's hand would have meant Rod's death.

Rod was imagining Junior holding the gun when he suddenly realized that Brad was talking to him.

"Hey, buddy. Snap out of it!" Brad said this loudly. He was moving Rod's right arm from fully extended to a folded position, then back to extended.

"I'm sorry. I'm having a hard time keeping my thoughts here," Rod answered.

"Well, here's a piece of news that ought to get your attention."

"What?" Rod asked.

"I just felt pressure from your right arm!"

Rod could not believe what he just heard.

Brad said it again, nodding. "You pushed back."

Rod looked at his arm. "Try it again."

Brad pushed very slightly, still holding up Rod's right arm from the elbow. Rod concentrated and then he realized he was moving the right arm. It was minor but he definitely knew it was his movement, not Brad's.

Brad said, "You see. That's you."

"Damn straight it is!" Rod let out a yell. "I got me an arm!" Rod immediately hugged Brad. "So, coach, what's next?"

"Hey, I think we keep doing the same things, just more on this arm. When you get enough feeling and movement we'll have you try to lift free weights. Maybe you'll get some of it back."

"Some of it? No. We're going for the whole shootin' match, son. As much as there is to get is what I want." Rod was as happy as he had been in months.

That evening dinner at the Retherford house started with a prayer of thanks. As far as Jim and Betty were concerned, the Lord had reached down and blessed Rod. The mood was sheer excitement during the meal. Afterwards Rod pressed Chris to do some resistance work with him. Chris was really happy to see his big brother making such incredible progress. "Hey big brother, pretty soon you and I can start going to the high school and use the weight room. I'm sure coach will let us."

"Chris, I'm ready whenever."

"I'll talk to coach."

After a moment the brothers hugged. This was a joyous day and Rod went to Patti's to share his incredible accomplishment and end a perfect day.

Finally Brad's work with Rod's arm had paid off. With each new session Rod was feeling improvement. However, forty-five pounds seemed to be a barrier for Rod and no one knew if his shoulder muscle would ever allow him to get past that weight.

14.

The Sunday that followed the day Rod started to regain his right arm, he joined the family, Patti in hand, and attended the Assembly of God Pentecostal service. The big rusty red church building was located east of town along highway 26. Rod and Patti walked to the steps of the church, her left hand in his right. That was a first since the summer before. They entered through a small vestibule that separated the front doors from the nave—the main room of the church. This interior space was divided into a pair of sections, each with fifteen rows of pews. The family sat in the fifth row.

On this day a congregation of one hundred assembled to hear Minister Milo Frankie. For Patti this day was her first to experience such energetic services.

The dividing line between Pentecostal churches and the mainline Protestant churches had been the first's form of religious experience highlighted by speaking in tongues, a sign of the so-called "Baptism of the Holy Spirit." In turn, that baptism was clearly described as the dwelling of the Holy Spirit in the individual believer. The gifts of the Holy Spirit included healing, prophecy, knowledge unattainable by natural means, and discernment of angels or demons.

Jim had come to realize that living life centered on that experience was as important as the experience itself. It was now something he discussed, and through his prayer asked for healing and help in all aspects of his life. Milo had introduced Jim to the essential theology—healing. The typical style of this he learned was a loud, forceful, expectation.

Historically, congregations that have practiced speaking in tongues have witnessed unusual trance-related phenomena. Visions, hearing voices, and unusual healings have often been reported. The Pentecostal Movement began at the turn of the 20th century with the "discovery" of the Initial Evidence Doctrine in the New Testament's Book of Acts. Over the years it has been challenged, and arguments both for and against its validity have been rendered.

The Initial Evidence Doctrine was, simply put, that the Baptism of the Holy Spirit was an identifiable experience in the Christian believer's life recognized by the inevitable accompanying sign of speaking with other tongues. "Tongues" are languages other than one known by the person receiving the experience, including the possibility of the language of angels, not only humans, as testified by the apostle Paul in his first letter to the Corinthian church. The experience was then supernatural in that one was able to do something that otherwise would not be possible.

The biblical basis of this Pentecostal teaching and doctrine was found in the Book of Acts as written by Luke. Acts is the second part of a two-volume work. In volume one Luke described Jesus' ministry and passion, and in volume two, also known as The Acts of the Apostles, he described events after Jesus' post-resurrection ascension to the Father. It was written circa 62 to 70 CE, after the apostle Paul's imprisonment in Rome.

During the service Patti and Rod attended, Minister Frankie asked for those wishing to dedicate themselves to the ministry to come forward for prayer. The first to come forward was a short, heavyset man named Ralph. George, taller and thinner, followed Ralph to the front of the podium.

Patti went wide-eyed when Ralph suddenly went down on the floor. Almost immediately, something hit George. He went face down, on the ground. George began to weep frenziedly.

Minister Frankie loudly stated, "God's presence is all over these two men."

Minister Frankie thanked God for this baptism in the Holy Spirit. As he said that prayer George burst out with, "And they were all filled with the Holy Spirit and began to speak in other tongues." And then George began speaking in another tongue for five minutes, as did Ralph.

Minister Frankie later explained, "If any of you haven't been baptized in the Holy Spirit, seek God about it and pray for it in faith. God never lets a thirsty soul go dry."

Later that afternoon Patti talked to Rod while they took a walk around the rodeo grounds. She seemed reserved about the Pentecostal spiritual experience. Though it all seemed hard to sign onto, she was clear in her desire to practice the Christian faith.

"Rod, please don't misunderstand me. I want to live a God-fearing life. But," she said, "I wasn't ready for the guys on the floor, that's all."

"Well, I don't know about guys on the floor, and speaking in tongues, or living in fear of God. But I believe my mom, and I know that prayer and spiritual guidance is what brought her through my brother's death. I want to have a spiritual life."

She thought about this for a moment.

"I do too. I want to have kids, so do you. I mean, we both want the same things. Why don't we stop talking about it and just get married?"

For Rod, this was a practical question and one he realized he should have asked Patti. It wasn't a question that started with flowers, romance, wild desires, dreams of greatness, but was based on mutual interests. The single influence that motivated him was his firm desire for children.

The following week Rod and Brad saw more progress. Rod could move his arm, raising and lowering it.

"You're close. I think its time for you to start with free weights," Brad said, proudly.

"Chris has cleared things with his coach so we'll start tomorrow," Rod added enthusiastically. "Brad, I don't know what else to say but thank you."

Brad nodded his head, a big grin coming on. In his thoughts the odds on this recovery were long. Fortunately for Rod Brad never bought into believing the odds as a prophecy.

Towards the middle of that week Rod was at the high school with Chris, daily. The old gym, chain used to lock the doors at night, had been converted into the weight room.

The brothers worked out after school hours, beginning with hand weights. Five pounds gave way to seven, to ten, and finally after another few days he made it to the empty forty-five pound bar. On his back, pressing towards the bar, he had to struggle to keep the bar level. His left arm wanted more while the right one could barely handle the stress. Chris would stand over the rack waiting to grab the bar to protect Rod. Forty-five pounds at that point might as well have been three hundred, and every set of reps was treated with caution since they both knew his condition was uncertain. Regaining strength was a positive sign, but the bullet was still sitting in between C-4 and C-5. How much stress would it take to cause that 29 grain object to move a fraction of a millimeter? That remained the lingering question for Rod.

In typical Rod fashion his enthusiasm did not waiver. Soon he was adding a pair of twenty-five pound weights and managing to press ninety-five pounds.

Christmas vacation had begun so Rod was going to the weight room both morning and afternoon, working with the weights. During the first week he pushed as much as possible, Chris joining him for much of this. Rod broke through a barrier making remarkable progress and was now benching one hundred eighty-five pounds. Once again, he seemed to hit another plateau. As hard as he tried he could not get beyond that number. Even Chris, a great believer in Rod, was wondering, was this to be Rod's limit? Even if that were the case Rod should be happy to have regained so much. Rod understood and appreciated that his little brother was trying to put a positive slant on something that could be a negative.

That evening Rod was quiet. Patti tried to engage him in talk about future plans but he was lost in a personal challenge. Rod was beginning to believe that if he could build himself back to his former size he would have a serious chance at returning to Washington State, not as a potential place-kicker, but as a defensive back. But how was he going to break the barrier?

Two days later Rod arrived at the gym in the mid afternoon by himself. The janitors were working on the hallways and had left the door to the gym open.

He began his daily routine. The warm up was the first priority. He would stretch, then take the empty bar and do fifteen reps. Then he would add the twenty-five pound plates and do six reps. Then he would double up on the twenty-five pound plates and do two reps. He completed this routine, placing the bar on the rack. He got up, grabbed two more twenty-five pound plates, slid them on the bar, and then added five more pounds to each side for a total of two hundred five pounds.

He sat down on the bench and studied the bar. Then he looked over to the open gym door. He walked to it, grabbed the chain off the exterior handles, pulled the doors closed and chained them locked from the inside.

He walked back to the bench and sized up the bar, those plates and the total weight of what he wanted to accomplish. The weight was not physical alone. That mass of steel held a key to regaining a future he had worked for. He was not going to let it defeat him. And he knew the time was now. If he had a prayer of a chance to get back on the team it had to be in the next semester that would start in a few weeks.

"Bull-shit." This rang out in the empty gym. "Damn bull shit Retherford that you can't get that bar up." His elbows went to his thighs and he put his head down into his hands. Holding his head he spoke again, this time answering Rick. "I know this is not smart big brother. I know. I know. If the weight is too much I could get pinned to the bench. But what the hell, I'm pinned right now if I don't go for it."

Rod knew if he did not get the two-oh-five up, somebody could find him later with a bar on his throat, lifeless.

He looked up at the bar again. "I could try for one eighty-five but what's the use. If I'm gonna fight for it, I'm going for the two-oh-five. So quit your worrying."

It was in his blood. Rod had been an athlete from his toddler years. His dad and Uncle Tats spotted it right away. Rod had faced tens upon tens of major obstacles, some of because of his small size, some because of his attitude, and some because of the cards life dealt him. What was resting on that rack, what gravity needed him to overcome was now a matter of his mind. Rod was convinced that the his body would respond, if he could wake it up to where it was before the fateful gunshot.

He thought about the day four years before when he was out of high school, working with his dad hauling trash. They passed the high school football field on a run to the dump and Rod was gazing at the team practicing.

He turned to his dad. "Sure am glad I got to play in those days. I don't imagine I'll ever have the reason to suit up again."

Jim responded immediately. "Why not play college ball?"

Rod's expression turned incredulous. He was used to his dad being the diehard optimist, but this was a case where he could not possibly be thinking about the reality or odds of someone wanting him to play.

"Dad, there ain't gonna be any colleges knocking down the door of a five foot four inch kid. What are you thinking?"

"Well son, you can enroll in a junior college. They have football teams. And the boys playing at those schools come from high schools, just like you do. You're as tough a competitor as any boy. So, why not? I know you can do it—if you really want it. You just walk on."

It was another of those moments where Jim Retherford had the opportunity to inspire his son to reach for the dream. In that moment Rod could not believe any of his dad's suggestion had a breath of a chance.

Rod took his position on the bench, laid back and reached up to the bar. He took a pair of really deep breaths getting the oxygen into his muscles. Then he lifted that bar off the rack. The left side came up but he had to really force the right side up. As he did he again wondered what was going to happen when he brought the bar near his chest to start the press upwards. He cleared the rack and with a shaking right arm brought the bar to his chest. The left side went up with some effort. The right barely moved up. The bar was now at a forty-five degree angle.

Rod concentrated on his right hand. He was telling his arm to put thrust to that hand. He struggled and the right side began to rise. He let out a loud and major grunt continuing to push. He pushed, and pushed, and pushed some more. Sweat was beginning to run off his forehead and into his eyes, stinging them. The right side was within one inch of locking out to complete the lift and Rod grunted again with a final effort that would either bring him a major personal victory or cause a complete collapse in his life. In the next five seconds Rod Retherford returned the two hundred and five pounds to the rack. He had done it.

He laid there, tears of joy coming to his eyes and then he spoke. "Thank you, big brother. We did it." He took another moment and then he sat up adding, "Thank you Dad for always encouraging me. Thank you Mom for guiding me. Thank you Chris for being with me through this. Thank you, Brad, for not quitting. Thank you Patti for your nurturing way. And thank you God. You have been listening, I guess."

After a few moments Rod got up, took another look at the bar. He put his hand on those weights, sliding his fingers over them. One by one he replaced them to their rack. Then he put his right hand under the center of the empty forty-five pound bar. He put his left hand on the bar too, but only to steady it. He curled his right arm, slowly lifting the bar. Then he replaced it.

"Done." Then Rod walked to the door, unchained it, stepped outside and proudly closed the gym door. As he walked to his car he said, "Go Cougs."

Rod and Patti were married in John Day, Oregon on January 11, 1981, at the Assembly of God Church. Milo Frankie was the minister and some three hundred people were in attendance.

15.

An eighteen-wheeler rolled into John Day at sunset, heading west. The driver turned north off the main highway onto the residential lane that led to the Retherford house. It was January 20, 1981 and Rod was beginning to see real progress with his right arm. The family was functioning again, out from the cloud of depression. Jim was advancing with the ministry studies with Milo Frankie.

The shoulders of the mountains cradling the town were deep purple as the western sky mirrored the last minutes of the day's sun. The icy breeze, always returning at this hour, would own the air until the earth made its rotation and welcomed sunrise again.

The driver was happily listening to a news story the world had been waiting for: "Tehran freed the US hostages after four hundred forty-four days," was the headline. The last fifty-two American hostages held at the US embassy in Tehran for more than fourteen months had arrived in West Germany on their way home to the United States.

The hostages had stepped from the plane onto the tarmac at Wiesbaden airport, tired but elated after their four thousand mile flight from Iran. Some of them gave the V-for-victory sign.

Iran had finally agreed to release the hostages after the US said it would release assets frozen in American and other banks, including the Bank of England, since the embassy was seized.

Former president Jimmy Carter, appointed as President Ronald Reagan's special envoy, had flown to Wiesbaden to welcome home these people on behalf of the country. The former president had been unable to broker their release during his time in charge at the White House.

Stories of the "abominable treatment" these men and women suffered at the hands of their Iranian captors were beginning to emerge. Letters from home had been burned in front of the hostages, there were regular beatings, and some talked of games of Russian roulette.

As the big rig came to a stop across the street from the Retherford's, the driver let out a celebrating holler adding, "Let's hear it for the Gipper!"

The driver was Dennis Adkins, early twenties. Looking at the hands, forearms, and neck from a street-side vantage one could easily see that he was robust. Dennis turned his view towards the house but his gaze went directly to Rick's car. His face had character, earned from taking on life—scars of an earlier period when little of the conventional was held sacred. Dennis' eyes softened as he took in the Galaxy 500, and a time lived before came up in this thoughts. He climbed down from the rig sporting cowboy boots, Wranglers, and a winter vest. He walked to the Galaxy, a slow grin revealing memories that wagon could share.

Every small town has a renegade, that guy or girl that doesn't fit in, the one that upsets the status quo. During the late 1960s and into the 1970s the social backlash to the war in Vietnam gave hippies a lot of attention by the media since they were largely considered outcasts. The images pushed at those tabloid consumers were that of longhaired teens wearing fatigues or bright colored prints from India—pot-smokers who were dodging their national duty by burning draft cards or fleeing to neighboring Canada. While some violated laws and stimulated violence, many were peacefully expressing opinions—utilizing their right to protest.

In redneck America, those red states and regions on a political map—an area generally made up of everything in between the West Coast of California and the north and southeastern shoreline of the country, the image of a hippie was as low as it got.

In the words of the once popular motion picture actress Mae West, "He was so low he could walk under my closed door without taking his top-hat off." In the context of her movie that gave us this humorous line, smiles came to many faces. But the low-life connotation concerning hippies brought out something other than humor. In the film *Easy Rider* Dennis Hopper and Peter Fonda were part of the hippie generation and ultimately paid for that with their on-screen lives in redneck America. The free and enlightened meet the illiterate was the suggestion of that film's final scene.

On the other political extreme, the intelligentsia of the blue states and regions—the densely populated Midwestern pockets that shared the blue moniker, had as limited an understanding of the people of the red states. These conflicting and often false impressions led to a myriad of generalizations that shed no real light on the people of either label.

Cinema has the power of affecting many and influencing thought on issues. *Midnight Cowboy* was a title that had made a major impression in 1970. It was an ultra-realistic adult film shot in New York City with sordid, downbeat and serious content. One of the two lead roles, played by then newcomer Jon Voight, was a character from Texas who pretended to be a cowboy in order to attract the women he hoped would pay him for his sexual services. It was X-rated and was the first such rated film in the history of the Academy Awards to win the Oscar for Best Picture of Year. To the men of the red states where one would be most likely to encounter the true cowboy culture, the Voight character of Joe Buck was labeled a "Rexall Ranger," or drugstore cowboy. He was a "wanna-be" cowboy.

This period was a time of change. The country was replete with an establishment that was threatened by the hippie culture. Images everywhere raised discomfort levels for each extreme, from radicals in Berkeley to the horror of the May 4th, 1970 killing of four protesting students at Kent State University in Ohio by members of that state's National Guard. This phenomenon dominated the general conversation. After the Kent State massacre eight million students, from middle schools all the way through college age, protested with a strike.

John Day, a community of hard working people of the land, like many communities, had its local outcast who gained the label of hippie. He was Dennis Adkins. He was damn proud of the fact that he annoyed everyone with his presence. Dennis was one of those who would have considered Joe Buck from *Midnight Cowboy* to be a drugstore cowboy.

A stout kid, Dennis was about Rick's age but short like Rod. He drove a motorcycle, wore fatigues, had long hair, and was generally viewed as a scourge, a blight on the peaceful town. No doubt to those who saw *Easy Rider*, he conjured up images from that film.

This is not to suggest that Dennis was pure innocence, for standing in front of the Galaxy that evening in 1981 he would readily have admitted that were it not for his time with the Retherford family he may very well have ended up in prison for any number of his youthful stupid attacks. Teens have those moments that defy adult logic to one degree or another. But, standing in front of the old sedan he was thanking Rick for being his buddy.

The theme song from *Midnight Cowboy*, "Everybody's Talkin'," with lyrics by the late Fred Neil, say much about Dennis.

Everybody's talkin' at me.
I don't hear a word they're sayin',
Only the echoes of my mind.
People stoppin' starin'
I can't see the faces,
Only the shadows of their eyes.
I'm goin' where the sun keeps shinin'
Thru the pourin' rain,
Goin' where the weather suits my clothes.
Bankin' off the northeast wind,
Sailin' on a summer breeze,
Skippin' over the ocean like a stone.
Everybody's talkin' at me.
I don't hear a word they're sayin',
Only the echoes of my mind.
And I won't let you leave my love behind.

In the early '70s Dennis and his family had moved back to John Day from Yreka, California. Both he and his mom took jobs at the Ye Ol' Castle restaurant. Rick was a coworker, and though they barely spoke, they were aware of the other. Dennis was wearing the hippie label at that point. Rick figured that the scruffy demeanor and testy attitude were on the surface. He also concluded that Dennis was far from being worthy of the population's collective disdain. Yes, his bad attitude and drinking had stimulated fights. Rick somehow understood that Dennis' traits developed from feeling incapable of being a part of what was considered normal.

The friendship began as the two were leaving work on a cold winter evening in 1973. Rick was drawing down on a beer and unlocking his Galaxy as Dennis passed by, his feet crunching on the snow and ice. They exchanged a friendly, respectful nod. Though Dennis was short Rick had imagined this guy could go twelve rounds with anyone. But in that moment Rick had something gnawing on his mind and maybe Dennis was someone he should become acquainted with.

Rick followed up the friendly nod with a question, "Hey bud, want a beer?"

"Sure, after eight hours in that kitchen don't mind if I do." As cold as it was outside, the beer was just what Dennis wanted.

Rick tossed Dennis a beer from his iced down guitar case in the trunk. Dennis took note of the guitar case and laughed.

"Damn, that's quite a deal you got there." Then, without hesitation Dennis popped the beer open and chugged it. He tossed the can to a nearby trash bin.

Rick asked, "You want another?"

"Naw, wouldn't be right to drink all your beer."

Rick accepted that and followed with, "Want a lift?"

"Yeah. Thanks."

The two climbed in and rolled off. Rick turned up the radio volume as Johnny Cash was doing his number one hit, "A Boy Named Sue."

"Johnny Cash at San Quentin. Hot Damn!" Rick loved the tune.

Dennis slapped the dash and agreed. "Damn straight." Then Dennis looked around the Galaxy. "Nice car. And, great wheels."

"Yeah. I likes her."

Rick took notice of the parking lot at the Chevron as they rolled past it. This was a car hangout in the evenings with lots of locals lined up behind the station, even on winter evenings. Rick made eye contact with a group of boys standing by a 50-gallon drum that had some wood burning. It was throwing up a pretty good lick of flame. Two of the boys were brothers. Mark, the older one, pointed to the Galaxy as it passed the station parking lot. Dennis noticed the reaction but said nothing.

Rick asked, "So, where to?"

"The other side of town."

Rick nodded. "No problem, but I want to pick up my brother on the way. He's down the street here."

Rod was waiting at the curb in front of the Retherford home. He hopped in, saying his hello to Dennis and shaking off the cold air. Then he got down to business without any hesitation, seeming anxious.

"So you got Dennis coming with us to the Chevron, Rick?"

"Naw. Just giving him a ride home," Rick answered.

Dennis bit. "What's happening at the Chevron?"

Rod jumped in before Rick could answer. "Couple a guys wanting a fight. They got something they need to prove."

Dennis responded. "Looked like more than a couple of guys to me."

"You were there?" Rod asked.

Dennis answered. "We just passed it. I saw five, maybe six guys paying a lot attention to this car."

Rod said nothing but Dennis could smell the wood burning as Rod was calculating the odds.

"What are you guys doing?—Walking into something stacked against you?" Dennis asked sincerely.

Rick spoke up. "Mark thinks he's a badass, gonna whup my little brother. Over my dead body!"

It was quiet for a few seconds as the car stopped for a pedestrian. The Chevron was about one block ahead, at an intersection with a traffic light. Dennis looked over at Rick who had his eyes on the road and was certainly thinking strategy. Then Dennis looked back at Rod who was staring straight ahead.

"You guys got friends coming to this, get together?" Dennis inquired with a chuckle.

Rick looked over at him. "You wanna even the odds for us?"

Dennis did not hesitate. "What took you so long? Nothing I'd like more right now then to flatten some hot-head."

Rod liked this a lot. "All right! Bring it on."

Rick was getting close to the station. He reached over and offered his hand to Dennis. And, they shook for the first time.

Mark and his friends were tossing down Mickey's Big Mouth malt liquor by the fire. He saw the Galaxy as it rolled towards the intersection. Mark bolted towards the car, followed a few paces behind by his five friends.

The Galaxy was stopped at the light as Mark approached at a good clip.

"Rod Retherford, get out of the car so I can kick your ass!" Mark yelled. His approaching friends were getting wound up and were shouting encouragements.

Rod started to open the rear door of the car but Rick barked, "Hold on, Rod. Wait till he's at the door then kick it open on his legs. When you hit him, land his jaw. And don't stop till he falls down or runs." Then Rick put the Galaxy in park.

As Mark hurried his approach Rod got his legs set to kick the door open. Dennis and Rick had their hands on the door handles and were ready to bolt into action.

"This is gonna be fun." Dennis was really looking forward to the approaching action.

The car was stopped about four feet from the curb so Mark had to step onto the pavement to reach the door. There was ice right where he stepped off the curb, and he hit it dead center. His face went from his loud mouth challenge to panic as his legs went right out from under him and he slid halfway under the car.

Rod and Dennis had the best view and could not believe their eyes. Mark was scrambling and slipping on the ice trying to get his butt out from under the car. As he did his panicked eyes made contact with a laughing Dennis.

"Rick, step on it," Dennis said. At that same instant Dennis raised his right hand and gave Mark a little wave goodbye, mouthing the words, "Bye-bye."

Rick could not tell that Mark was under the car. He dropped the Galaxy into gear and rolled forward as Mark was still trying to get out free on the ice-coated pavement.

As Rick began rolling forward he was watching the other five guys backing Mark. They were about on the car, and two of them were carrying lumber—rough ends of two by fours that would work as clubs. Instead of waiting for them to get to the car and bust a window, he wisely took Dennis' suggestion and rolled around the corner.

Rick felt and heard a loud clump not realizing that he was rolling the rear wheel of the car over Mark's legs.

Rod was watching and could not believe what just happened adding, "Shit!"

Dennis burst out laughing. "Damn, son, you just rolled over that big mouth's legs. Shut his ass up, I'd say."

Rick said nothing, just grunted. In no way had he intended to run anyone over.

Mark's friends were in disbelief as the car cleared past its victim and rounded the corner. Their fearless leader was now looking at his legs, in total shock. And in further amazement everyone watched as Mark got himself on his feet, turned and walked back towards the fire. He was walking and no one can understand why or how to this day. It was certainly an accident and fortunately no bones were fractured, only egos that deserved to be, were bruised.

Rod wildly added, "Rick, I can't believe what I just saw. You rolled over that asshole, and now he's walking."

Rick continued down the street adding, "Whatever. Guess the fights over."

Dennis piped up, "I'm buying. Stop down there at the liquor store. What a way to start a Friday night."

From that point on the Retherford boys and Dennis were like brothers. Indeed, Rick liked Dennis when no one else would give him the time of day. Rick saw through the camouflage of attitude and hair to the great soul and wonderful wit that inhabited Dennis. After that night they were fast friends. Being the same age they did a lot more together than with Rod. These two had no mercy picking on each other, teasing, laughing, and loving what life offered them.

Rick essentially adopted Dennis and brought this big puppy home to the family. Within days of their first handshake Dennis cut off his hair, gave up the fatigues, and adopted the look of the cowboy.

Having bonded with Rod on that first evening he was completely welcome. Dennis had a lot of meals with the Retherford family and all the boys were family. Dennis had a serious interest in rodeo, having a cousin who was doing pretty well competing. The Retherford's gladly introduced Dennis to the sport. And to his benefit at this time, Dennis was under the watchful eye of Jim who had become a surrogate father to the once hippie kid.

Among the many things Dennis learned during those wonderful days was Jim Retherford's clear requirement for family loyalty. Every time the boys would head out, whether day or evening, Jim reminded Rick to watch out for his younger brother.

His eighteen-wheeler secure, Dennis walked into the living room being warmly greeted by Betty, Jim, and Chris. Still filled with nostalgic thoughts of the days in Rick's car he gave Rod a bear hug. After chowin' down on some of Betty's country fried steak and some catching up on his life, the family left Dennis and Rod to do some talking. Dennis sat in amazement hearing about the bullet that almost took his buddy's life.

In their minds what they had done together in the years after Rick's death, was the stuff of legend. He told Rod it was no surprise that Rod Retherford was sitting in front of him, alive and walking. Dennis knew if anyone on earth could survive the odds of being shot in the neck, it was Rod.

This was a night of memories for both men. But more importantly, Dennis realized that there was a larger purpose in this walk down their history's parallel paths. Rod needed to use the total sum of his knowledge of what he had overcome in those earlier days, to remind him that his current challenge was just that—another challenge along the journey of life.

When they turned in for the night Dennis thought about Rod going through, just another challenge. "Damn" he said to himself. "Them's easy words to say Adkins, a lot harder to do."

16.

The news of the release of the hostages was lighting up millions of lives. The morning after Dennis' visit Rod helped Jim hang the American flag while at the same moment Betty and Chris were tying a fresh yellow ribbon around the tree in the front yard. She had replaced that ribbon several times over the preceding months, always believing that those folks would come home.

Yellow ribbons were being tied around trees everywhere in America in support of the hostages coming home. The whole thing was started by Penne Laingen, wife of Bruce Laingen, U.S. charge d'affaires in Teheran. Ms. Laingen has said she was inspired by the song "Tie a Yellow Ribbon Round the Ole Oak Tree," written in 1972 by Irwin Levine and Larry Brown and made famous by the popular group, Tony Orlando and Dawn.

However, Betty and Jim Retherford remembered another song, "Round Her Neck She Wore A Yellow Ribbon." This song had been popular for decades. Some say it was sung during the War between the States. Betty and Jim remembered it from one of John Wayne's classic westerns, the 1949 release titled, *She Wore A Yellow Ribbon*.

As Rod drove across town later that morning the visit with Dennis was still very present. Some of what they laughed about was replaying, those wonderful stories of self-generated insanity they had managed to survive. Rod was laughing out loud thinking about some of their antics while he was driving.

Shooting pheasant on the Seely ranch was one of those crazy moments no one might believe. Jim and Melvita Seely had met Rod competing in the rodeo. They had a daughter, Cecilia, who was Rod's age and who also competed in the girl's events. During Rod's high school years they had dated a little during the summer month's rodeos. Cecilia had an attribute that really appealed to Rod at the time. She was four feet eleven inches tall and she made him feel taller. Her family had given her the nickname Ceily and Rod enjoyed calling her Ceily Seely.

The Seely's were generous folks and Rod was always welcome at their ranch. It was one of those afternoons, Dennis and Rod both carrying .22 long rifles as they hunted ground squirrel. This was sport. Back at Rod's grandparents in the Midwest, the Freeman's, hunting tree squirrels was for eating.

Pan-fried tree squirrel with biscuits and gravy was one of Rod's favorite breakfasts, a tradition passed down from his grandmother. She and his maternal granddad lived in the Ozarks, near a little town, and operated a dairy farm on the rolling hills. Rod had the best memories of his younger days on vacations, hanging out with his granddad. The property had two little ponds 40 feet across where they would go frog gigging or hook catfish to bring to Grandma for dinner. Rod would laugh every time he thought about Grandpa Freeman, dressed in bib overalls, one strap over a shirtless shoulder, unlaced low-top leather boots, and a bag of Redman chaw pressing out of his rear pocket. He liked to drink peppermint schnapps but had to hide this from his disapproving spouse. Every where on the property that Rod would walk while following his granddad there would be a bottle of peppermint schnapps hidden. The chicken pen, the tractor toolbox, and in the barn, there was always another bottle. And, with every stop granddad would have a nip of schnapps. And, each time he would offer a nip to Rod.

On that hot afternoon on the Seely ranch Rod and Dennis were bummed out because they were having no luck spotting any ground squirrels. They were talking about giving it up for the day as they pushed themselves up a slight grade along a streambed cut by rain fed erosion. It was that time in the afternoon when the air was still, and the flies were plenty. Dennis had removed his cowboy hat to swat a fly that was making him nuts. He wiped his brow with his forearm and replaced the hat just as a pheasant broke from its cover. It took flight one hundred feet ahead crossing their path. Rod heard the flutter, spotted the bird, as Dennis raised his .22 and drew a bead, then squeezed a shot off that dropped the pheasant.

"What? What was that?" Rod said in absolute amazement. "You have to be the luckiest SOB on the planet."

"There was no luck in that, 'cept for scaring up the bird," Dennis answered with a little John Wayne swagger.

"Bull shit!" Rod stopped as he said it. "You ain't gonna get away with telling me that wasn't dumb luck."

"I'm telling you luck's got nothin' to do with it, Bud."

Rod continued up the grade and noticed a bumblebee flying a figure-eight over the wildflowers along the shoulder.

Pointing up the grade Rod said, "Watch me shoot that bee out of the air."

Dennis looked, spotting the busy bee. Rod raised the rifle and squeezed off a round from twenty yards away, and the bumble-bee dropped. This time Dennis was in shock. He said nothing. They walked up to the flowers, Rod leaned over and picked up the critter by its one remaining wing. He held it up and examined his kill.

"Damn. Look at that. Guess that makes me the winner." Rod exclaimed, along with an irresistible chuckle.

Dennis was shaking his head. "Okay. I gotta admit, that was one hell of a shot." He took a step and added, "Blind-ass luck—but one hell of a shot."

"How can you call that luck, asshole? I called the shot!"

Rod strutted on as Dennis grumbled to himself.

Rod recalled that tale as he was driving across John Day on his way to kick footballs. Truth was, there was only Dennis to share these stories with. It would take another guy just like this friend to appreciate moments they shared. And, the truth of the matter was—who would believe that these two guys could make those shots unless they were witnessed? Maybe it was a good thing that there was only one Dennis. John Day may not have survived another Dennis, or Rod.

Later in the afternoon on the way home from his weight training at the high school Rod drove to the Grant County Drive-In Theater wanting to revisit a memory. Seeing the marquee brought back a host of memories again, most with Rick and Dennis. Rod turned in the entrance to the empty lot and circled until he was in the middle, facing the direction of the refreshment stand that was located opposite the screen. He stepped out of the car and walked to the front of his car, leaning back against it. He could almost see action from the early '70s with Rick and Dennis.

Not all of those times were about laughs. Rick and Rod's relationship with Dennis was pushed to the redline on an early June evening in 1974. The drive-in was the location where it happened.

Summer nights in John Day start late, and that contributed to the popularity of the drive in with the teens. The theater generally showed a double feature, the first beginning between 9:30 and 10:00. This would put the second show's end at 1:30 to 2:00 AM. For the high school crowd wanting to be out late on Friday and Saturday nights, this was the perfect excuse.

Rolling in early enough to get a good parking spot, and then checking out the scene was the standard routine. On this evening Rick was driving his Galaxy and Rod was sitting in the middle of the front seat since they had picked Dennis up on the way there.

Rod was cleaning his nails with a three-blade pocketknife he had been given. He was making as much out of this as possible by closing the blade, then opening, then closing, then scraping under a nail, wiping his fingers on his jeans, snapping the blade closed, then after a few seconds reopening it and repeating the entire exercise. Rick was watching the ladies, almost oblivious to Rod. Dennis had been the same, but there came a moment when the knife and Rod began to annoy him.

"Hey, let me see that thing," Dennis said.

"Can't you see I'm using it?" Rod replied.

"Yeah. You're using it to annoy the shit out of me," Dennis responded.

Rod kept up with the routine, opening and closing the knife, occasionally cleaning under a nail. Dennis looked out over his right shoulder trying to dismiss this irritation. But Rod pressed him.

"You like my knife, Dennis?" he asked as he snapped the blade closed again.

Dennis kept his attention outside for the moment without answering. But Rod extended his arm in Dennis' direction to admire the knife. And in that moment Dennis could not resist the impulse. He snatched the knife from Rod and with his right hand took it outside the window, faking a toss, but actually resting it on the gutter above his door.

"Give me my knife back, Dennis." Rod said, while not believing the fake toss.

Dennis shrugged. "It's gone."

Rod opened the palm of his hand. "Give me my knife back," he said again.

"I said it's gone."

Rod turned to Rick who was now paying attention to what was developing.

"Rick, I'm gonna hit him in ten seconds if he doesn't give me the knife."

Rod knew without a doubt that if things went into a fight that by his dad's mandate, Rick would have to fight Dennis. And so Rod figured he had nothing to lose by pressing the matter.

"One, two, three." Rod counted off the seconds. At six Dennis once again said, "I ain't got the knife."

"Seven, eight, nine,"

And on ten, Rod landed a left hook on Dennis' mouth, the hit cutting his lip. Dennis was a little surprised by the hit.

Rod piped up again, "Now, give me my knife."

Dennis got past his momentary pause in a heartbeat, snapped his left arm around Rod's head and placed him in a headlock.

Rod began struggling with Dennis' arm trying to pull it away from his head but the grip was ironclad.

Rick knew he had to step in, and quickly. Dennis was likely to pop Rod.

"Shit." Rick slammed his open hand on the dash. "Dennis, don't hit him, or I'm gonna have to fight you."

Dennis knew that Rick meant exactly what he said. If they fought it could change things between them forever. After a few more seconds Dennis let Rod go.

In that moment Rick could see that Rod was about to take another swing.

Rick added, "Rod, give it up."

Dennis needed to walk it off so he stepped from the car, tossed the knife back to Rod, and walked to the concession stand. After a few minutes cooling down, things returned to normal. By the end of the first film it was just another night of fun.

The next day the boys were at the Rodeo together. Rick helped Dennis prepare himself for his first saddle bronc ride. Two weeks later would be Rick's last rodeo.

A few months after Rick's death Dennis rented a trailer from the Retherford's and that became his home. It was parked out front of the house. Dennis truly became Rod's brother and they each filled in for the loss the other felt with Rick's death. They roamed together, whether rodeoing, fishing, hunting, chasing the girls, or whatever. As did Rod, Dennis had his time working at the Hudspeth Saw Mill. Weekends would arrive and it was rodeo time. They would drive through the night on Friday to make it to the Saturday morning contestant's check in, ride in their respective competitions, party during the night, get up and shake off the hangover to compete again on Sunday, and then drive back to John Day and get right back into their Saw Mill jobs.

When there was no rodeo event Rod and Dennis would invent their own excitement. The Firecracker Scramble is perhaps the most notable Friday evening inspiration from Rod and Dennis. No doubt there are some John Day men who remember it well. There may be a few of those men who would like to know who was responsible too.

This was no Fourth of July celebration. It was, however, the evening of July 16, 1976, and these two cowboy pranksters were looking to shake things up around their sleepy hometown.

Their target was along the main highway that entered the town from the west. The Den, a local watering hole, located in the basement of the Sunset Restaurant, sat on the edge of the road. A creek ran along the property and a bridge with one lane to each side of the road spanned the draw. Diagonally across from the restaurant, just across the bridge, was a dairy that typically had milk trucks parked in its front lot during non business hours.

Before describing the Firecracker Scramble know that the country was unnerved about two stories that had been in the press. One was a prophecy of sorts, the other was about a massacre. John Day being an agricultural area the cover story from *TIME* magazine's July 12 edition had gotten a lot attention. "The Bugs Are Coming" cover featured the title graphics in a style much like the opening title to George Lucas' *Star Wars*, with a particularly mean looking insect crawling towards the words, and thus towards the reader.

The essence of the story was: "Now, however, all over the U.S. and in many areas around the globe, bugs are on the march, relentlessly not only retaking the ground so recently won by Homo sapiens but also making new advances. Aided by Government restrictions on pesticides as well as their own growing immunity to the chemicals, and benefiting further from the miscalculations and complacency of their human enemies, insects seem well on their way to fulfilling the chilling prophecy of The Hellstrom Chronicle: 'If any living species is to inherit the earth, it will not be man.'"

The other story had the nation glued to television sets on Monday the 12th also. A custodian at the California State University, Fullerton campus, had shot nine people in the basement and first floor of the library with a .22-caliber rifle. Seven of the nine wounded victims died.

Edward Charles Allaway, had opened fire shortly before 9:00 AM, when the library was scheduled to open. The victims were his fellow university employees. Allaway fled the campus after the shooting and drove to a nearby hotel where his wife worked. He called police and confessed to the shootings. Police arrested him and found the .22-caliber rifle in the back of his car. He was subsequently represented by a public defender in trial proceedings and pled not guilty by reason of insanity.

He was later found guilty of six counts of first-degree murder and one count of second-degree murder. However, a second phase of the trial determined that he was not sane. Five different mental health professionals diagnosed him with paranoid schizophrenia. He presented a history of mental illness. He was committed to the California state mental hospital system, where he remains at Patton State Hospital in San Bernardino.

Allaway's apparent motive was that he thought pornographers were forcing his wife to appear in movies. This served to enrage him. His wife had filed for divorce just before the attack occurred. The defense alleged that commercial pornographic movies were being shown by library staff members before opening hours, but Allaway's wife was not in them.

With the Fourth of July having just passed, Rod and Dennis happened to have a bag of firecrackers in their possession. They hatched the idea of tossing the bundle of lit firecrackers down the staircase so that the rapid explosions would sound like gun fire and that would scare the bar crowd out of their wits.

Indeed, the plan was put into action. The lit bundle was tossed and landed right at the door to the bar. Dennis and Rod ran as fast as they could on that diagonal line across the bridge to the parking lot in front of the dairy. They took up observation spots under the trucks expecting to see panic-struck drunks stumbling over each other as they ran for their lives.

The exploding firecrackers did sound like rapid gunfire. Shortly after the last explosion, instead of watching comedy unfold, Rod and Dennis watched twenty-five very angry men come flying up the stairs and begin a search for the culprit. Those guys were not finding any of this amusing.

Rod looked over to Dennis, a grin plastered ear-to-ear. "Those boys boiled up out of there like a band of Apache's on the hook."

An angry voice yelled, "Find them bastards, sons of bitches."

One of the bigger men yelled out, "Asshole. Whoever you is, you gonna die!"

The more of this Rod and Dennis heard and saw the more they laughed. Within the group Rod spotted a friend, Loren Porter, who was a big old cowboy. Loren was directing some of the younger guys to search along the creek.

Rod turned to Dennis. "You see Loren."

"Shut up Rod! Want to get us killed, you lunatic?" Dennis said in hushed tones. But no sooner were the words spoken and Dennis began laughing himself, his hand over his mouth to silence this uncontrollable reaction to the comedy across the road.

The boys watched as the twenty-five pissed off guys checked both sides of the creek, all around the building, inside every parked car, and as far as they could see up and down the road. Since no one heard a car driving away the men figured the culprit was on foot. Two of the younger guys were convinced that whoever did it was in the creek, so they kept searching down there cursing all the way.

Amazingly enough none of these men ever considered checking across the bridge. For five minutes Dennis and Rod had the pleasure of watching the patrons of the Den search in all the wrong places. Finally there was a collective shrug as they gave up and returned to the bar.

Rod and Dennis waited a couple of minutes to make sure they were in the clear. Then they cautiously moved to their car. They barely drove off before the two of them began to howl. This scene was the funniest thing they had ever seen, and they were very proud of the fact that they created all that hysteria.

After forty-five minutes of driving around Rod and Dennis were so curious they had to go to the Den, walk in, and see what things were looking like.

The bar was looking pretty normal when these two strolled in, trying really hard not to grin too much. They contained themselves while getting a couple of sodas. Rod spotted Loren, and being that he was a friend, this gave Rod a reason to let a grin come out as if he were really glad to see him. They sat down at the same table, Rod grinning and Dennis trying to contain himself.

"Loren, how yah doin'?" Rod said this with what Loren immediately detected as an unusually broad smile.

"I'm fine." Loren was looking back and forth measuring the looks from each of these boys.

"So what's happening around here? Seems kinda quiet for a Friday night?" Rod suggested.

Loren did not answer right away. He settled into his seat, leaned back on the rear legs and then spoke.

"It was you two."

Rod tried to paint a question mark on his face but Loren knew him too well.

"What are ya talkin' about, Loren?" Rod asked.

"Don't even try that, with me, Rod." Loren was now shaking his head.

Dennis tried to sell it too. "Yeah. We just were driving by and stopped to see what was going on here."

"Uh huh. Sure you were." Loren leaned forward and motioned with his finger for the boys to lean in. Then he added, "If these guys figure out it was you two, you won't get out that door. Now I suggest you don't wait to finish your drinks there, but you just get up and leave."

Rod tried to convince Loren once more but he was cut off before he said the first word. "Leave now. It ain't gonna be pretty what'll happen to you."

The boys looked at each other in agreement and quietly made their exit. As they walked to the car the amusement of all of it had worn itself out and they were now glad they had survived the prank. Inside the car, away from the threat of being heard they relaxed and the anxiety of the bar faded. As they drove away they began to giggle. Then they laughed, uncontrollably.

Rod pulled up to the front of the house as Chris was coming home from his Grant Union basketball practice bouncing his ball as he walked. They met up on the sidewalk. Chris was now a shade taller than Rod.

"Hey little brother. Looks like you're a little taller than me now. What you think about them apples?" Rod asked with a grin.

Chris tossed the basketball to Rod. "You're *my* big brother."

"And proud of you."

"Sure was great to see Dennis again. He's so much fun," Chris said.

"Yup. That's the truth."

"So, you coming to my game tonight?" Chris asked.

"Does the sun set in the west? Of course I'm coming."

At that moment Betty opened the door and called them to dinner. The Retherford's were eating early because of the game that evening at Mount Vernon high school. This was a family that never missed the opportunity to support their own. On their way in the house they talked about Rod's progress with the weights. He was up to two hundred and fifty pounds. It was a slow gain but still encouraging.

The family said a prayer before beginning dinner thanking God for their blessings, praying for the well-being of the released hostages, asking God to bless Rick in the afterlife, and to help the Retherford family with the life that was ahead of them.

17.

The basketball game was at the high school in Mount Vernon, a little town ten miles west of John Day. Rod had driven Chris to the school after dinner and walked with him to the locker room where the Grant Union Prospectors were dressing. It was warm in the enclosed space filled with metal lockers, wooden benches, cotton towels, athletic shoes, uniforms that never let go of the stench of the sweat from the previous wearing, the Bengay analgesic heat rub, and the medical grade adhesive tape being wrapped around many of those teen ankles. These familiar odors were comforting to Rod and he took all of it in.

"Man, this is like a homecoming for me. I miss the locker room," he told Chris.

"A homecoming? It's a locker room, Rod." Chris laughed at him, not mockingly though. He loved his big brother and found inspiration through Rod's example and unbending dedication to sports.

Chris added, "You know, I'll bet if you looked up diehard in Webster's it would list 'Rod Retherford' as the first definition."

Rod laughed with him. "Webster's huh. That's pretty good little brother." Rod turned for the door and added, "Dunk one for me."

Chris watched Rod as he gave his respectful hello to the coach who was just entering the locker room. Chris admired the rapport Rod had, his way of acknowledging the coach. By this point in Chris' young life he knew that his own love of sports, athletic challenge and competition, would propel him into college. He had discussed this with Rod who was an example to him, and a constant encouragement.

Rod lingered by the door as the coach began drawing a play diagram on the blackboard at the end of the room. The white chalk was making X's and O's, and all those meandering, circuitous lines and arrows that translated into action. This got the team's attention.

"Okay guys, listen up." The coach had a spiral memo tablet in his left hand with a few stats he had noted, and he referred to it with a gesture as he began speaking. "Whatever these guys are coming at us with, we are sticking with man-to-man defense. You boys better hit that court like it is your last chance in life, like it means the big ticket that gets you the prettiest girl in school on your arm at the prom. I want you to make your grandparents proud, and your sisters, and your brothers . . ." Coach was looking at Chris at that moment, ". . . your parents proud, all your relatives, and ancestors proud! I want them jumpin' up and down proud! I want all the former Prospectors and the faculty proud! And I want you to make me proud! But most of all I want you to make yourself proud! Do you understand what I am saying?"

The response from the boys was in loud unison. "Yes sir coach."

He held a cupped hand to his ear and repeated, "Do you understand what I am saying?"

This time the response burst from the boys. "Yes sir! We understand!"

This level of enthusiasm brought a smile of satisfaction to the coach.

"Okay. Okay. Now its time to ask the Lord for his blessing." The boys looked surprised. They were not accustomed to the coach praying. The room turned silent as all the boys lowered their heads.

"God. I know I ain't much of a praying man. But I hope you are willing to listen now. The boys are coming up against an opponent that's real tough. My boys here have worked hard. They're good boys, most of 'em at least." He rolled his eyes as he looked towards heaven.

A couple of elbows jabbed teammates, but the mood abruptly turned serious again.

"Lord, and any of you saints that care, sometimes we make mistakes when we're playing. And just maybe, from where you're sitting, you can see that comin' before it happens and could tip us off. If you could maybe help our boys be a little quicker off the boards, get them on those rebounds faster. And maybe you could be reminding them to pay attention to my signals from the floor. That would be a real nice thing."

The coach dropped his head for a moment of silent prayer. Then he said, "Okay, lets go crush these guys."

"Now, I'm going out to check in with the scoring table." He added with a sarcastic flavor as he turned for the door, "And, make sure you tie your shoelaces."

The boys were laughing as the coach walked out talking to

Rod. The two passed a few memories back and forth on the way to the court. As coach shook hands with the two officials for the game Rod continued to the bleachers. One of the officials was short, a little overweight, and bald. The other had a basketball player's long body.

Jim and Betty were sitting center court with Patti, about five rows up from the floor. As Rod joined them the Prospectors made their entrance. As much thunder as the two hundred excited fans could generate filled the gym. The boys ran in a serpentine line that extended to the basket at the north end of the court. They began the lay-up and free-throw warm up routine while the cheerleaders worked the crowd from the sidelines.

During the first half Chris played well, and the Prospectors held an eight-point lead. Chris had lots of encouragement coming from the home fires.

As the first half progressed Jim was getting increasingly annoyed with the shorter official's calls from the floor. His vocal level was rising with each comment he shouted to the court. Making his words even more penetrating was his deep, gravelly tone. Of course, Betty and Rod had lots of experience with Jim and paid him no mind, but for Patti this was new. Rod reassured her several times not to be embarrassed.

Chris had been distracted by his dad's loud commentary a few times. At one minute before halftime while the team was circled around the coach during a timeout Chris was once again distracted by his dad.

Coach barked at him, "Retherford, are you with us, or do you want to join your dad yelling at the stripes?"

Chris turned to the coach, "Sorry."

Coach took a second, then continued. "You boys need to set

the pick and roll, run it at them. Drive these boys. And work for the good shot."

The Prospectors went in for that final minute and played as if possessed by all those saints the Coach prayed to in the locker room. They managed to gain another two on the scoreboard. In the first half Chris scored fourteen points, highest on the team. Three of his steals he took to the other end of the court, laying the ball against the backboard right on the mark, but with a smoothness that almost seemed like slow motion.

During halftime the coach did his best to make the boys believe that they could turn this game into a blowout. The boys truly believed him. So after the Gatorade or ice water, and the cooling of their red-hot skin, the Prospectors vacated the room and charged back to the arena where they fully intended to humble their opponents.

The second half was an intense replay of the first half. Chris worked the guy guarding him with an uncanny instinct. He scored on two straight turnaround jumpers, converted two more steals into points, and was fouled three times. The Prospector's lead was growing. That was until two minutes before the end of the third quarter. From Jim's perspective his boy had been fouled at least seven times and he made no bones about this with the short official. It mattered not that the Prospectors were winning. Jim had a bone to pick with this man of authority.

Jim's displeasure finally brought him to the floor. The fact that anyone might be watching him, that he might somehow be embarrassing his son, or his family in the stands, was not a thought that passed through his consciousness.

"Hey stripes, are your eyes connected to anything inside your bald head? Or are those two BB's on each side of your nose just rolling around inside an empty skull?" Jim was on the edge of stepping onto the court.

Chris' coach was shaking his head, not knowing how to quiet him. He feared the consequence would be a team distraction that could turn their lead into a loss.

The other official called a timeout and stepped up to Jim suggesting a change. "Sir, if you would please sit down."

"Somebody's got to keep you guys awake!" Jim responded.

"If you spent more time watching the game then worrying about our calls, things would probably work out just fine for everyone. Now please, sit down." The official walked off not interested in the response to his request. This was not a coach he could throw out. This was a fan and all the official could hope for was the man taking his seat so the game could go on in an orderly fashion.

Both teams were huddled up. The Prospectors reviewed a play that would have Chris bring the ball into play.

Coach looked up to Chris, "Retherford, you gotta play the game. Ignore the crowd. Ignore the noise. Play the game!"

As Chris readied himself for the inbound pass he was watching his dad again, praying that he would sit down. He passed to his man, stepped in and the ball was passed back to him as planned. However, Jim was on the official before Chris reached half court. Chris did not hear what went down, but the short official blew his whistle and stopped the game. The official wheeled around in the direction of Jim and marched over to him, removing the whistle from around his neck.

Jim was not afraid of a conflict and at first thought this guy was going fisticuffs with him. From Rod's vantage he wasn't sure what was about to come down and prepared himself to come to his dad's aid.

Betty was trying to make light of all this and turned to the woman next to her saying, "Jim gets so involved. He just loves sports."

The woman forced a smile. As far as she could see, Jim was a loose cannon that should be tied down. By the time the short official reached Jim he had removed the cord around his neck that the whistle was attached to. With an outstretched arm he offered the whistle to Jim. Jim just looked at him.

The official pushed the whistle at Jim. "Here. You take this. You think you can call the game, have at it."

Jim took the whistle. "You bet I will. And I'll do a darn sight better than you."

Aside from many things that might have deterred Jim, his cowboy boots were perhaps the most obvious. As he clumped onto the court and proudly blew the whistle, the team members and the fans could not believe what they were seeing. This man who had nothing kind to say to the officials was actually taking over, walking onto the court wearing a pair of boots. To all watching this was a show worth paying money to see. On the other hand, if Chris could have, he would have vanished.

The short official conferred with his associate and both coaches, and the principals of both schools before walking out. They all agreed that the game would continue since so much of it was already in the books.

So, the play continued, but the attention of the fans was clearly on Jim Retherford and his cowboy boots. After two sets of plays that caused him to run each length of the court four times, with the clump, clump, clump of his boots being the most dominant sound and fully distracting, no points were scored. Mount Vernon's principal could not accept this boot noise. He went to the scoring table and had the clock stopped.

The principal walked up to Jim at the sidelines. "Sir, you cannot officiate this game. Your boots! You can't wear boots on the court."

Jim calmly nodded. "You're right." He reached down and to the surprise of the principal who had hoped to stop him, Jim pulled off his boots and set them down. Then he blew his whistle and said, "Lets play."

Jim would go the balance of the game in his socks.

While this new plan defeated the noise issue it created yet another dimension to what was rapidly becoming a circus environment. As play resumed Jim quickly realized he could not stop himself on the highly waxed floor surface. As he would run from end to end, picking up speed, he would find himself sliding towards the baskets at each end of the court. Back and forth, sliding the last fifteen feet towards the basket, Jim actually began having fun. Fortunately, the crowd was so amused that they did not boo him out of the gym. Jim Retherford was skating and this was turning into an ice ballet on a basketball court. The graceful play of the athletes going up for the lay-ups, making coordinated offensive passes, contrasted to Jim skating alongside side the action.

There was not a single person in the gym that could have imagined such a sight. Rod too began to enjoy seeing his old man out there calling the game, sliding from one end to the other, taking a position like a skier, a skater, or surfboarder as he would glide with the action. Even Chris began to laugh at the spectacle.

In an amazing way, Jim turned the game into something everyone enjoyed, just once. When all was said and done, the Prospectors won the game in a blowout. Chris walked up to his dad after the game and asked, "Well dad, did you enjoy yourself? You looked like you were having fun."

"Sure as heck did, son." Jim was all smiles. "You played a great game. I'm really proud of you."

Betty told Chris how great he played, how happy she was they won, and she even commented about the people sitting next to them, how impressed they were with his shooting. She managed to thoroughly avoid any mention of Jim's behavior, almost as if he was not there.

On the way home Patti and Rod laughed about the site of his dad running back and forth, first clumping, then sliding.

Patti asked him, "Hon, when we have kids, are you gonna do that?"

"I doubt it. But you know what. I love my dad. He put his money where his mouth was tonight. He wasn't going to let the official embarrass him. He took on the job and he did all right."

"I sure noticed that he didn't hesitate to blow the whistle and cover the game," she added.

"Main thing was, he was there for Chris. And when we have kids, I'll be there for them. Whatever it takes." Rod was sounding adamant. "Whatever that means, I'll do what I think my kids need."

Patti agreed. "Long as it's the right thing to do, I guess."

Rod said no more. But he kept thinking about his dad. There was not another father he knew that would have taken on that official's bluff. Most times, he thought, people have too much invested in how things look. The beauty of his dad, and he really saw it the gym, was none of that stuff mattered. It was what was going on inside his kid's hearts and souls that mattered.

Jim had always been the first to say, "You can do it." On this night someone had said that to him, but not as an encouragement.

The official said it to intimidate the parent heckler. To the official's surprise, and everyone in the gym besides Betty, intimidation was not a key that would turn Jim Retherford off. To the contrary, it lit him up.

This experience linked to something else in Rod's thoughts. From his days wrestling he learned to use the momentum and body weight of his opponent to his advantage. Taking a body in motion, the force of that mass, and redirect it so that the moving body played to his advantage was the trick. Short, lightweight Rod, had flipped many an opponent on their backs using the momentum and weight that the opponent had put in motion.

In some way, he realized, his dad had just done that brilliantly— only thing was he did it emotionally.

"You know Patti, my dad's a good man. He may not seem to be the brightest light in the room. But don't let that fool you."

This comment made Patti uncomfortable. "I'm not saying nothing about your dad, Rod. I was just wondering about what's gonna happen when our kids are going to Grant Union. That's all."

"Well, first of all, I don't know that our kids will be going to school here. I'm not sure about where we'll be living. Second, I really believe all parents can do is the best they know how."

It turned silent for a few blocks. Patti kept her eyes directed to the passenger side of things, not sure whether they were having a disagreement.

Rod finally spoke again. "You know, there's probably not many dads out there that trust in their kids as much as my dad."

"Rod, I ain't saying nothing bad about your dad," Patti snapped back.

"I ain't saying you did. But I want you to listen. I wanna tell you a story."

She folded her arms, realizing that the best tact in the moment was to let Rod speak.

"When I was eighteen my dad got himself a brand new pickup truck. It was a pretty thing and it was a big investment for my folks. Dennis and I were used to borrowing dad's old truck and we didn't think nothing about asking him if we could borrow his new one. He said yes. We were just going for a daylong fishing trip to Canyon Meadows. You ever been up there?"

"The reservoir, ten miles past the high school, right?" she answered.

"Yeah. So we take the new truck up to the lake to fish. We get set up but it's pretty cold. So we decide to build a fire. But it starts to rain. All the wood we can find is wet. But Dennis and I are determined to catch a fish, we just need to find a way to stay warm."

Rod began to laugh as he remembered the story. "Dennis got the bright idea to siphon a little gas from dad's new truck so we could get the firewood lit. We had no way to get a hose into the gas tank, but we did have a coke cup. Dennis figured if we loosened the rubber gas line leading to the carburetor, stuck the end into the coke cup, turned the ignition on and cranked the engine over so the gas pump would push some gas into the cup, we'd have ourselves a campfire. See, Dennis figured that if I could just click the ignition, you know—on and off as fast as I could, that we'd get the cup full of gas."

He laughed out loud. "So we get all set up. He's got the cup in hand, the rubber gas line is now in the cup, and he tells me to click it over. I click it. The engine does a split second crank. He yells good—got us a half cup. Now do it again, real quick. So I get ready, twist that key over to give it that little click. Only thing is, when it turned the engine, it backfired. It was so loud and such a surprise, Dennis jerked back and the cup spilled over on the engine.

Next thing we know the gas ignites and we have ourselves a fire, not at the campsite, but on the engine of dad's brand new truck. I'm talking a barbeque raging on top of my dad's brand new engine."

Patti is now turned, facing Rod, and carefully following this crazy story.

Rod continued. "Well this fire goes from a little flame to a full on fire in two heartbeats. Dennis and me are running around trying to figure out how to put out the fire. It takes us about a minute to get the flames out, but not before the front end of dad's new truck is blistered from the heat. The tops of the fenders, the hood, and of course, inside the engine compartment, are all burned up. And, with the rain that's been falling getting heavier, Dennis and I are getting pretty wet. Now we go into survival mode asking ourselves, "what do we tell dad?" If we tell him what we just did, hell I wouldn't have blamed him if he kicked us all the way out of the state. So we needed to figure out a story that made sense. The truck wouldn't start so we have to leave it. And, we were too embarrassed to ask for a ride. So we gathered our stuff, locked it in the truck and walked up to the highway, turned north, and walked the ten miles home, in the rain. By the time we got home we had concocted a story that seemed to be our only salvation from dad's temper. And this is the point to me telling you this whole long and crazy tale. We had cooked up a big lie. We told dad that something must have been wrong with the carburetor, it backfired and caused the engine to catch fire. When we told him, leaving out any word of the real story, he believed us. He did not doubt our word for one second. Dad said he'd contact the insurance company and he was sure they would take care of it. The insurance company did send out an adjuster. He looked at the truck and agreed that it must have had a defective part. The entire damage list was paid for by the insurance company so dad got his truck back, like new. But the whole thing that has stuck with me is that dad never would have thought his kids would lie. That's really the kind of man we're talking about here."

"But you did lie?" she asked.

"That's not the point. The point is his trust." Rod took a second then continued. "A couple of years later I told him the entire story and apologized for misleading him. He surprised me when he said he always wondered about that story. But he also explained that he was a kid himself and he understood what boys will get themselves into. So, not only did he really know what was up, he chose to trust, and he also chose to understand. Those are two qualities I hope I have for my kids, Patti."

Patti said no more, just reached over and took Rod's hand.

18.

During the final weeks of January 1981 Rod had pushed his weight training to the point where he bench-pressed two hundred sixty-five pounds. Along with muscle development he had brought his weight back to one hundred seventy-two pounds. In his mind he was now ready to make a return to Pullman, physically and emotionally. It was time to walk into Coach Walden's office and say the magic words, "Coach, I'm back. Sign me up. Give me the scholarship, and lets play football."

Rod knew it would not be quite that simple, however. The school would certainly require a thorough medical examination. With the bullet lodged in his neck would one of the doctors say, "We cannot permit Retherford to play," as a part of a review of the medical file? Or if the doctor did clear him to return to the field, what would happen the first time he went up for an interception, got tangled with the receiver, was hit in midair and put into a cartwheel motion, striking the ground head first with a two hundred pounder landing on top of him? There was only one way to get the answers to those questions. Whatever the outcome, Rod was going for it in his customary fashion—pedal-to-the-metal.

So, on the first day of February 1981, Rod and Patti waved goodbye to the family from their overloaded car and rolled north towards Pullman, Washington. He had notified the WSU admission's office that he was returning as a married man, that his wife was enrolling, and that they needed student housing. He had put together enough cash to cover the first two months of rent—seven hundred dollars. They would apply for HUD housing allowance, hopefully that would be approved and a rental unit would be available within the first sixty days of the semester.

On the road Rod and Patti talked about what was ahead of her. She had the athletic ability to join the women's volleyball team and Rod was encouraging this. For a small town girl, taking the leap to a major university was very intimidating. He knew that she would make friends through athletic competition and that would help her integrate into this new lifestyle. He explained that he was going to be wrapped up in football, classes, and working to earn the money they would need to live on, so Patti would need to be self-motivated.

All the talk about what Patti would encounter those first days in college brought Rod to remember what led up to his first days at Treasure Valley Community College. The school was located in Ontario, Oregon. This chance to advance his education by attending college happened through rodeo. Rod was a successful high school competitor who continued with the sport after graduation. Treasure Valley noticed him and offered a tuition waiver in the fall of 1978.

Two years before, the summer of Rod's high school graduation, he and the family traveled to Sulphur, Louisiana for his competition in the high school nationals. Having made it into this select rank for competition against the best from each state was a tremendous accomplishment. Rod loving football so much had been curious about the city of Sulphur from the day he read about the famous Steeler quarterback Terry Bradshaw's days in high school. In 1965, competing for the state championship in Sulphur, Terry's visiting team from Shreveport, the Woodlawn Knights, lost to the Sulphur Tors 12-9, but Terry was such an outstanding athlete he earned a spot in *Sports Illustrated* "Faces in the Crowd." And Rod knew well that Terry was the first player selected in the 1970 NFL draft. How an unknown goes from defeat to recognition, and then earns a shot at the big time was a mystery that Rod wanted to solve. But for now he was a competitor in a rodeo event that was another step forward—a ticket to a new experience.

Rolling along the highway to Pullman, watching fence posts and power lines pass, the image of the back seat view from the 1976 road trip—the family pulling a trailer across the southern route during the hot June weather, became as fresh as his thoughts about dinner the night before when the Retherford family said a farewell prayer for Rod and Patti.

For young Rod, Chris, and Mitch Greg who had also qualified in saddle broncs, the humidity of Louisiana was a new experience, but until arriving at Sulphur the enthusiasm did not wane. Rod was remembering how excited thirteen-year-old Chris was being with his big brother, the young teen anticipating good times with Rod, his very own rodeo star.

In Sulphur, quite naturally and understandably, Rod spent most of his time hanging out with his rodeo peers. This deflated Chris since he spent his exciting vacation to Sulphur mostly in a hot trailer with his mom and dad. This was not quite what the boy had imagined during those thousands of miles of highway that passed before his eyes traveling east. However, watching Rod compete lifted his spirits and gave him a payoff for all that anticipation.

For Rod, it was an experience that further confirmed that nothing would happen unless he reached for what many might say was impossible. How many high school cowboys made it to the nationals as a bareback rider? Not many. How many got there at five feet four inches? Even less. One experience, whether it brings victory or defeat, leads to another attempt. Later, Rod took his ambition further and won the bull riding title for the Five Western States Association. Competition, strange places, new faces, it all became a routine. Every step along that path had prepared him for the unknown that was to unfold at a time and place of destiny's design.

What Rod could not realize during those years, however, were the thoughts running behind the watchful thirteen-year-old eyes of his brother. Every one of big brother's steps were being observed, measured if you will, by Chris. And this was building a drive within the boy, causing development of his own passion for sports. Ultimately, Chris excelled to such a level that he entered college on a basketball scholarship.

Rod rode rough stock on the Treasure Valley College team his first year. In rodeo terminology, rough stock riders were the ones competing on the bucking saddle broncs, the bareback broncs, and the bulls. The other events such as roping were timed events and those competitors were known as *Timey's*.

There was a theory Rod grew up with, "if you were right handed—you rode left and, of course, if you were left handed—you rode right." Over time Rod had learned that the sport was split between successful athletes in each event, bareback, saddle bronc, and bull riding, and that some rode left without regard to being left-handed, and some rode right, without regard to being right-handed.

One old cowboy had told Rod to walk along the top of a wall holding up the alternate arms. When the more comfortable arm was figured out, then which hand to ride with would be known. Strength was a reason for going with one hand over another. But the better alternative was to get in shape.

By twelve years of age Rod knew that the American-style bull rope could be used either left or right-handed. And, he also learned how important it was to make sure the rope being used was laced properly for the hand to be ridden with. The purpose of the leather lacing in a rope handle was to keep the handle from turning over. When a rope handle turned over, the rider's closed fingers would be pinned between the bull's back and the palm of the rider's hand. And, if the hand could not be opened—the rider would be hung up, not able to get loose.

During the first of his Treasure Valley Community College years Rod was at the height of his self-destructive path that carried him away from the pain of Rick's death. His use of marijuana had elevated to the point where his daily nighttime routine, the last thing he did before going to sleep, was to load his bong for the next morning. And indeed, at daybreak after turning off the alarm clock, he would sit up, grab the bong and light it, drawing that smoke into his lungs so he could start his day. After having his breakfast, morning shower and readying himself for school, Rod would load the bong again and anesthetize himself. He would carry a reefer to school that was the size of a cigar. The object of the exercise—stay stoned every waking hour.

This habit of getting stoned became so outrageous Rod actually would compete with himself to see how quickly he could smoke his way through a pound of Sensemilla, one of the strongest varieties of marijuana available to him. Rounding off his habits at this time, Boone's Farm Wine or Strawberry Hill wine coolers. To a degree, his young body and mind could tolerate some abuse. However, there was coming a point when his course may reverse, but it would be too late for what short allotment of youth he had remaining.

Rod came out of his memories to the present as an automobile on the approaching lane suddenly drifted off the road at sixty miles per hour. As its right side wheels bit into the soft sloping shoulder the sedan flipped, throwing up a dust cloud. The other cars slowed on both sides of the highway. The sudden change woke Patti.

"What's happening?" She asked.

"Somebody must have fallen asleep at the wheel. They just rolled off the road."

"Oh my God. They could have hit us."

Rod was slowing to turn around and see if he could help the victims of the accident. Waiting for the oncoming lane to clear he saw a State Trooper's sedan approaching and knew he no longer needed to offer help. As the slowdown cleared they continued on and Patti returned to her nap.

Falling asleep at the wheel was one of those hazards Rod had come to deal with during his years of chasing the rodeo. And, perhaps he had a guardian angel on his shoulder named Rick. Rod was so familiar with being stoned he knew he could manage most routine tasks. His propensity for marijuana in all forms had been revealed to the family as a result of a weekend visit that Chris had with Rod during the first year at Treasure Valley.

His first months at school, Rod was living just across the river from Oregon in an apartment in Fruitland, Idaho. His roommates were Mary Wright, Patti's sister, and the girl he used to date Ceily Seely, now a good friend. They had cooked up a tray of marijuana-laced brownies before Chris arrived with his friend, Greg Josi. They were spending the weekend with big brother Rod. Hungry off the road, the two younger boys dove into the brownies.

Chris asked, "What's the weird green stuff in the brownies?"

Rod responded wryly, "Oh, just some healthy greens." The truth was—these were seriously potent.

Greg was enjoying the sweets but Chris did not care for the taste so he quit after one bight, not without making the comment, "Man, those taste like shit."

Rod chuckled. The choice of words was ironically perfect. He imagined that as it had happened for him late, Chris might not have had any exposure to grass, as yet. He opened the refrigerator and asked, "You boys want a coke, some milk, a Mickey's Big Mouth?"

"I'll take a Mickey's," Greg called out. Chris joined in on the request.

Later on the boys went to the basketball court to shoot some hoops. Chris was okay, not feeling any high. Greg was another matter. He was looped. Rod could not hold back the laughter as he watched Greg passing his hands in front of his face in slow motion. Greg was very slowly saying, "Man, my hands. This is like watching TV. Things are just going down."

Rod finally admitted that the brownies were not innocent sweets. He was so amused he spontaneously added, "I made them with Tequila." He knew his mom and dad might find out about this, but it was part of growing up as far as he was concerned.

Chris did not know how to deal with this. It was funny to watch Greg spacing out, yet his fundamental and pure athlete's mind did not cotton to the idea that his big brother was lacing the food with Tequila, or marijuana. Chris had learned early on from the spectrum of examples provided in his formative years, to understand the positive and the negative in any situation. Rod had been a huge inspiration through his sport accomplishments that defied his physical size—that unbending determination to do what was deemed impossible. At the same time Chris had observed Rod develop reckless and dangerous habits. There was a lesson in that that registered as the younger brother made his pragmatic choices. This moment was one that Chris took as just a moment in time, not a reflection of what he knew was the true soul of his big brother.

That evening, after Greg recovered, he took the boys to a local dancing club. Rod had the best time watching his tall, good looking, but terribly shy little brother be absolutely stunned by how many good looking girls there were under one roof. Though he remained to himself most the night this was one of those moments that told Chris there was a lot more to life than John Day could ever offer.

When Rod received his tuition waiver and started college Betty was hopeful that he would find his way past the dangerous habits. To her disappointment the substance abuse had increased. After hearing a little from Chris about his weekend with big brother Rod, Betty was worried about him influencing Chris. As a member of a small community isolated from the sprawling urban areas of the country where drug abuse was more often seen, Rod's habits became a great fear of hers. In Betty's thoughts marijuana use was likened to what the more exposed urban dweller might believe about heroine addiction. The specter of another potential life tragedy with the Retherford children weighed heavily on this spiritual mother. She was close to her own emotional meltdown with Jim's continued anger at God for the loss of Rick.

Betty could take this destructive behavior no longer and demanded that Rod sit at the kitchen table with her on a Saturday afternoon so that she could confront the issue. She was prepared to take him to the mat, a term he knew well from wrestling, in order to defeat the devil that was controlling his behavior. Betty's own vice with cigarette smoking had elevated as a result of the emotional trauma that made up the previous four years.

As those miles to Pullman ticked off the odometer, Rod could see his mom chain-smoking and drinking coffee with a shaking hand. She had looked at him with tears streaming from her eyes.

"Son, this evil habit you have, the marijuana smoking, is going to ruin your life. You will become property of Satan himself. You are throwing away every single thing you have ever accomplished with the drugs you live with."

"Mom, smoking a little dope is no big deal. Everybody I know at school does it."

"I don't care about everybody. I care about you." She took another drag. "Birds of a feather flock together, Rod. The friends you have chosen are certainly not the healthy ones if they all smoke marijuana."

"Smoking a little weed is no worse than drinking. In fact its probably better for you," he insisted.

"Well, I've seen you drinking too much also. And its not a little bit either. I look in your eyes when you're home and all I see are saucers. You're becoming an addict."

Rod laughed. "I'm not using heroine mom."

Betty began to cry. She put her head in her hands and wept, releasing the building anguish. She mumbled "God, tell me what to do? I want to save my family."

Rod heard the prayer. It gave him pause to think about what he was doing. The grass smoking was not only affecting him, it was now touching the lives of those he loved. It was clearly not as simple as "Just getting a little high."

Rod studied the ashtray where Betty's cigarette was resting, its rising line of smoke leveling off in a flat strata of the kitchen atmosphere. The burning ember was touching the collection of butts and ash that filled the tray. Even though he smoked dope he did not like being in closed spaces with cigarettes burning.

"Mom, I don't want you in any more pain. Since we lost Rick its been hell for all of us. Maybe you are right about me harming my life. I think everyone of us, maybe 'cept Chris, has been acting out, like you and those cigarettes. When I was a kid you smoked, maybe a half-pack a day. Like me with the grass, we've both gone too far. See, I know those cigarettes of yours are doing you no good." He reached out for her, to get her to look up to him. She wiped her eyes, took another drag, and then looked at her boy.

He paused for a moment while finding his way to a decision. "I'm going to quit smoking the weed. Right now, from here forward, that is my pledge to you."

Relief began to register on her face.

Rod continued, "But, Mom, I have one condition to that. You have to promise me that you will quit smoking cigarettes. Those things are going to kill you."

He kept a steady gaze at her as she thought about the commitment it would take on her part.

Rod gently asked, "Will you do that, Mom?"

She began to nod. "You turned the tables on me, son. But I guess its only right that you would ask me to do as much for myself as I'm asking you to do."

She reached out and took his hand. "Okay. Deal."

He smiled. "Deal."

That was the last day either of them smoked.

19.

Rod and Patti made a pit stop along the Columbia River, grabbed a burger and hit the highway again. She fell asleep shortly after they left the restaurant and Rod went back to his memories, those miles of life he had covered. It all certainly led him to Pullman, and now for a second time.

After the smoke and haze cleared from Rod's mind, and having finally come to terms with Rick's death, he regained ambition. Playing college football became the order of his life. As he considered walking-on at Treasure Valley he remembered how crazy he thought his dad was when he had suggested this idea two years earlier. Beyond his choice to forgo anesthetizing himself daily with Sensemilla loaded bongs, in those two years Rod's physical height had increased to five feet ten inches and his weight was at one hundred sixty-five pounds. He was no longer feeling like a runt, was no longer living with the knowledge that he was a pothead, and he had some serious accomplishments in rodeo to encourage and inspire him. So Rod walked-on to Treasure Valley's football team.

His first step was to inform the head coach of his intent. Ron Kulm had earned his masters from the University of Idaho, having played college football there as well. Rod knocked on the coach's office door. Ron, deep in paperwork, looked up and invited Rod to come in.

"Coach, my name's Rod Retherford."

"Hi Rod. I'm Ron Kulm. What can I do for you?"

"I wanna play football." Rod stated this with absolute resolve, and strongly enough that the coach believed him.

"You have any experience, Rod?"

"Played in my senior year in high school. Also my freshman year," Rod answered.

"Okay. What happened to the two years in between?"

"I was told I was too small." He said it with a certain challenge in his tone.

Ron shifted in his chair. He immediately knew there was a story behind the words "too small," but the question in his thoughts was, "Do I really need to know?" After a moment Ron asked, "And what year student are you?"

"Sophomore," Rod answered.

"You just decided to play football again? Why now?"

"I decided to make some changes in my life."

It almost seemed to Ron that Rod was impatient. That could be enthusiasm, his desire to have a chance at the team, or it could be the attitude of a young man. Ron was becoming more intrigued and asked, "So you have little experience. And, what position did you play?"

"I'm a defensive back."

"Okay?" Ron was chewing on this when Rod interjected.

"You'll never find a player that will put more heart into the game, Coach. Will you give me a chance?"

It took Ron all of one second to respond to such directness and impressive presence. "Okay. Come out for afternoon practice tomorrow. Check in with Farny. He's the defensive coach."

Rod cracked a little grin, showing a sign of relief in at least having the opportunity. Rod reached out and shook the hand of the man who just gave him the opportunity to try out. That is all he wanted, the opportunity. "Thanks, coach. I'll see you tomorrow."

Rod passed Farny in the hallway. He had no way of knowing that was the man he would try out for the next afternoon. In Rod's customary cowboy way he made eye contact and gave the man a nod along with a "Howdie." This simple gesture of friendliness put Rod's face in Farny's memory.

When Farny walked in the coach's office, Ron was thinking about the brief conversation he just had with Rod. Before Farny said anything Ron spoke. "Hey Farny. There's a kid named Rod whose trying out at practice tomorrow. He's for you, a defensive back."

Farny nodded and was about to bring up his reason for coming to the office as Ron continued with, "There's something about that cowboy. See what you think."

Farny gestured over his shoulder to the hallway. "I think he was the one who just said hi to me."

Farny was Gary Farnsworth. He was in his late forties and had a world of experience coaching the young players. He had been Ron Kulm's high school football coach and was a big influence on Ron's entire career. Needless to say, the two men worked well together having a great mutual respect.

Farny knew that his players would usually arrive at the junior college level of football not knowing much about the game. Yes, they all had played high school ball. However, he knew that the obvious choices in ballplayer talent had already been grabbed by the big four-year schools. Farny and Ron had the unenviable jobs of shaping players out of "green" talent. Farny, being a man of country roots, knew that the green sapling can be bent—shaped in a good or bad direction. At the beginning of each season his hope was that the new crop was green enough so that he could develop them, rather than being faced with undoing bad habits.

The next afternoon, grabbing the defensive coach's attention first off was something that Rod knew he must do. And indeed, that's exactly what he did. Rod's attention getter the first day of practice: He ran the forty-yard sprint in 4.65 seconds. And, what made this a big grin moment for Rod, he had made a point of finding out that J.R. Smith was the man to beat. And he did. Most importantly, in his own mind—in one 4.65 second burst of the millions of seconds that Rod had been alive, Rod went from a first year junior college pothead to a second year football walk-on who ran faster then the team's fastest man. Not too "B-A-D" Rod said to himself.

After Farny and Ron watched Rod's tackling during a scrimmage, the way he wrapped up his man, and how he would stay just ahead of a receiver on a pass play, they both knew this kid was a rare find. They looked at each other revealing their disbelief after several more plays, now having seen Rod break up runs and defend really well against the passing game. Farny said, "And he walked in and just said, 'I want to play'?"

Ron was nodding. "Just like that. Darndest thing about him Farny, I knew he meant exactly what he said."

In the eyes of Farny and Coach Kulm, Rod Retherford had immediately established his ability to play free safety. Farny was a position coach. Ron completely trusted his longtime friend's instinct on players. Farny would play the best athletes, the faster and smarter kids, on his defensive squad. When the season began Farny decided to give Rod the starting spot at free safety and Ron was in complete agreement.

Rod was not the kind of young man that would put salt on someone's wounds, nor did he walk around carrying grudges. Most confrontations were either dismissed or settled in the moment. But the incident with his high school football coach snatching the life, taking the desire right out of his young sophomore heart, was a moment of painful disappointment that continued to live in Rod. On the day when Farny named the starting team, and Rod Retherford heard his name read off as the first string free safety, his chest filled with pride. This strong, tough as nails, schooled in the hardest way from experience, and determined cowboy, managed to hold back the tears as the rush of joy swelled. He called his mom and dad within minutes and passed on the great news. He thanked his mom for the courage she had to push him towards cleaning up his life. In her customary way she took no credit but shared his joy. He reminded his dad of the conversation they had a couple of years earlier when Jim had told Rod that he could walk-on at junior college. Rod admitted to his dad that he thought his old man was nuts at the time. Then he thanked his dad for always being so positive and helping him to believe in himself.

The first game of the Treasure Valley season was at Walla Walla Community College. Rod proved himself worthy with eighteen solo tackles. He showed no mercy when hitting and tackling. He was beaten up and bruised in this game because in reality, Treasure

Valley did not have a good team that year. They were especially weak on the defensive line. Their opponent's offensive backs would blow through the line of scrimmage untouched. Rod was fast, and despite the pain, he loved the challenge of the game.

Andy Mosby was a teammate of Rod's that year. There was an instantaneous connection between these two players. Andy was a tailback and so during scrimmages these two players were on opposite sides. Andy was five foot four inches tall, but was one hundred ninety pounds and built like a body builder. Rod could not help but thinking of Andy as a small version of the famous Houston Oiler's back, Earl Campbell. He had the same player quality. And, like Rod, he was fierce. Andy had the experience of being tackled by Rod and knew what a determined and fearless hitter he was.

Their friendship brought Andy to John Day for Christmas that year. He was the only black man in the county and became a curiosity at the playground. Kids watched as Andy, Chris, and Rod played some hoops. Andy was fluid and all over the court. These kids saw moves they could only have seen watching television. At one point, as the kids saw Rod complete a slam dunk, one of them asked, "Hey can you teach me how to do that?"

Andy became part of the Retherford family. Later, his football career took him to San Francisco State University from Treasure Valley. And, Andy was more than happy to return to John Day to stand for Rod as his best man for his marriage to Patti.

The Treasure Valley Chucker's season was almost as bad as it gets, one in nine. Rod played well but the simple truth, their defensive squad could not hold the competition. Amusingly enough Rod and Andy's favorite game that season was on the home field. Betty and Jim were present. Midway through the third quarter while both teams were huddled near the fifty yard line, a Treasure Valley student geek—with Go Chuckers written on his bare back with a black marker, attempted to streak down the stadium stairs and across the field, right down the line of scrimmage.

This action caught the attention of the entire stadium crowd. Going down the stairs he jogged right past Betty and Jim. She turned to Jim saying, "Why Jim, that boy's got no clothes on!"

Jim, who knew only too well what he had just seen, responded. "Yes dear. I saw that too."

The streaker, now moving across the field, was being observed by the players. Brad Cook, a wild lineman teammate of Rod's mumbled, "That's a moving target."

Brad broke from the huddle with about ten yards to accelerate. He lowered his head and blasted the streaking geek at midfield, dropping him to his side in a daze. The crowd was hysterical watching this. Brad got up from the tackle and walked back to the huddle as the streaker, dazed but still able to move, got up and continued to the other side of the field. As he climbed a cyclone fence the streaker was met by a waiting policeman who congratulated him on his run, then provided a trip to the police station.

At the end of the Treasure Valley season Rod was pumped about college football and quite convinced that he could play with any team. He went to Farny and asked him to contact Boise State University's recruiters and recommend him. It was an opportunity to play at a higher level in NCAA 1-AA ball. The Big Sky conference would give Rod exposure to more opportunities.

Farny did not feel Rod was ready—he had much to learn and another season at Treasure Valley would make him into an eligible candidate for the bigger programs.

Rod, though he really respected his coach, did not agree. Even with Rod's objection to Farny's position, the coach refused to make the call saying, "I don't feel right about making the recommendation, Rod".

Rod bit down hard. It would be inappropriate to be anything but thankful for all the good experience and quality coaching that Farny had given him. But from deep inside that voice came up in Rod and he internalized what otherwise would have been an outburst. "Here we go again. It's my high school football coach saying 'I'm too small.' Well, damn it, I'm not small anymore. I don't want to be told I can't do something! What I don't know I'll learn. Nobody will work harder." Those thoughts were covered in a microsecond and Farny was never to hear them. Rod thanked the coach for considering the idea.

Some say there are no coincidences in life. That night Rod happened to read a story about the legendary Paul "Bear" Bryant who took Alabama through so many successful seasons. Rod instantly saw himself walking-on to Alabama and playing for the Bear. Rod called his dad to discuss the idea.

Jim was quick to say, "Well son, you can do it, and I'll help all I can. We will at least get you there. Considering how hard I know you're working the rest will be in God's hands."

Coincidences continued, and this is where the events became no longer serendipitous, but actually more like a part of some larger plan. A student friend from Rod's freshman year at Treasure Valley, Mike Walker, called to check in with his former teammate, Andy Mosby. Mike was big, six feet two inches and two hundred and thirty pounds big. He was from Indianapolis, African American, had a silver front tooth, wore his hair in an afro, and was a hard-hitting player. Andy and Mike played ball together at

Treasure Valley the year before Mike was recruited by Washington State University. That year Rod and Mike met by chance outside a Treasure Valley dinning room. Rod was parked in his van listening to music, hanging back and grinning—smoke wafting from the open windows, and Mike happened by. Mike took a look at that friendly face and said, "Hey man, what's happening?"

A conversation broke out and the friendship began—the five foot ten inch redneck cowboy and the cool six foot two inch afro-topped black Midwesterner.

After Andy finished his conversation with Mike, he turned to Rod and said, "Hey, you wanna say hi to Walk?"

Rod was happy to check in with his old friend. The conversation came around to Farny refusing to make the recommendation to Boise State, and that he was thinking about walking-on at Alabama. When Rod mentioned walking-on at Bear Bryant's Alabama, Andy laughed out loud.

On the other hand Mike said, "Rod, what are you thinking? Why go all the way to the southeast when you could drive a couple of miles to Pullman and walk-on at WSU?"

"Can I walk-on there?" Rod had not even thought about the Cougars as a possibility. Sometimes things being so close are less obvious.

"Can you? Why not? They just recruited ten junior college defensive backs, some from Southern California, to fill vacant positions for spring football. Walk-on, Rod. I know you. You'll beat some of those guys out and become a Cougar. This is a happening school, man. You'll love it."

"Well, okay. I'll give it a shot. Thanks, Mike. Now, what do I do?" Rod asked.

"Call Coach Ken Woody in the football office. He recruits from

Oregon. He's also the kicking and receiver coach. He's the one who came to Treasure Valley and recruited me."

Rod took the lead and called Ken Woody. The call was fairly short but Ken seemed interested. He told Rod he would come to the college in the next few weeks and they would discuss the possibilities. What Rod did not know was that Ken was impressed with Rod because of what he had heard from his good friend, Bob Eberson, who coached Spokane. He had seen Rod knockout one of his players. He knew what it took to play in PAC-10 ball. The year before Ken had found Mike Walker at Treasure Valley and figured he might get lucky again.

Several weeks passed and Ken did arrive at the Treasure Valley campus as promised. Rod and Ken sat down while Rod took a break from his job as a fry cook at one of the campus restaurants. Rod had done a little homework and learned that Ken had played for the University of Oregon in the mid '60s. His first position had been as starting kicker, then he played as a defensive back, and as a wide receiver. His coaching experience led him to the Washington State University football coaching staff in 1978.

Ken had looked at game films and had seen enough of Rod to know that a meeting was warranted. He was very direct. "Rod, I'm going to tell you straight up. We don't like to recruit from junior colleges that much. You see, in high school you have four years to mold a player. In junior college we see kids that are half molded and usually with really bad habits. Sometimes they are fixable habits."

Rod knew better than to interrupt. Ken continued, "The game films are not the greatest quality but I can see that you can play. Tell me about your background in sports."

Rod kept his words brief. It was once again a situation where he wanted to get to the heart of the matter. He told him about high school, the disappointments and the victories. He told him about rodeo. That seemed to register positively on Ken. The quality that was really registering in that moment was Rod's directness. He was looking Ken in the eyes. Ken could easily see that Rod was not someone easily intimidated.

Ken then asked him, "What are you looking for, Rod?"

"The opportunity to play, coach. It's really that simple. To me everyday is game day. I play hard. I love the game. I want to learn more. To do that, I have to challenge myself so I've got something to rise to."

Ken liked the brevity of the answer. The truth was evident in Rod's directness. "We have a turnover problem. Our head coach, Jim Walden, is determined to build a team that can match the PAC-10 giants. We have a lot of confidence in our program. The Cougars have not been known for strong defense in the past few years but with Walden and the rest of us, that's going to change."

"Give me a shot at it. That's all I'm asking."

"Even though I couldn't tell from the film I think you may be a good addition so I'm inviting you to walk-on."

Rod's heart raced. He was just given a chance at the big time. And here he sat in his kitchen whites, sweaty and sticky from frying burgers at a little junior college in eastern Oregon, and he was talking about joining a PAC-10 football team.

Ken continued, "I can't offer you a scholarship yet. We have to see what you are capable of first."

Rod then asked very pointedly, "What do I have to do to get a full ride? You see, coach, for me to come to WSU, I'm gonna have to work. And, that's not a problem. I'll do whatever it takes. But I need to make my plans."

Ken really liked the question. He was not used to hearing about work plans when recruiting kids. Rod was a responsible young man looking to make full use of opportunity.

"If you make it to number two on the depth chart we'll give you a full ride. It's up to you."

Rod put out his hand to shake on the deal, his way of saying, "okay, I'll do it." Ken told him when and where to show up.

Patti and Rod rolled into Pullman late on the appointed afternoon and he introduced her to the campus. First and foremost, he walked her onto the stadium ground. As it had been for him, she was overwhelmed with the size of it. Then he took her to see the school mascot, Butch T. Cougar, and she heard how much it meant to Rod that brother Rick was represented to him in that name. After signing in at the admission's department they went to the housing department and received their apartment assignment. Rod confirmed that his application for HUD assistance was in process.

As they got to the car Patti hesitated. She looked at Rod showing an overwhelmed expression.

"This is so big. I don't know how . . ."

Rod interrupted to encourage her, "Patti, I had the same feeling the first time I saw this. If you get yourself on a team, everything will change. I just know it will."

With clear reservations in her thoughts they drove to the apartment complex. Rod would have no way of seeing past his own enthusiasm at returning, to recognize what Patti was forecasting with her words of doubt. Time would serve to reveal another conflict in Rod's developing life.

20.

Rod and Patti moved into a one-bedroom apartment on campus at Steptoe village. They had the barest essentials. A mattress on the floor for the bed, a couple of secondhand light fixtures, two folding chairs and a folding card table made their dinette set. Just as so many young couples make do, Rod and Patti readied their Spartan dwelling. By the time the car was unloaded it was too late to go to the football office. Rod would wait until the next day.

Jim Walden was on the phone in his office, turned in his chair with his back to the door. Rod was waiting just outside the open door and could hear the coach's phone conversation.

Jim's tone was forceful, direct, and he sounded a bit tired of the conversation. "Lets not kid ourselves here. When I was a kid I learned what manner's are. When asked a question I was taught to say, Yes, Sir, or No, Maam. I wouldn't dare have had an attitude. I did what I was told. And, my pet peeve, if you want to know, there was none of this treating them all the same B.S. If a kid's special, hey treat 'em special. They win an award, great. But this thing about everybody has to win, come on. Get them ready for life. We aren't living in a nursery school, for Christ's sake."

Jim turned around and saw Rod standing at the door. His face changed from frustration to a big Mississippi smile. "You know what, I got something important to do. Lets talk about this later. Bye." Jim put the phone down and came around from his desk saying, "Rod Retherford, you son-of-a-gun. How the heck are you?"

"Coach, good to see you."

They shook hands strongly. Jim was really happy. "So?" he asked with great anticipation.

Rod jumped right in eager to say, "I'm back. I'm ready to play."

"Now that is some great news." The coach had a very broad smile. "You got a big old heart, Rod—and, you have a great want-to." Want-to was a Jim Walden term describing a quality that he needed to see in his athletes. With his mission of developing a Cougar team that would challenge the stalwart PAC 10 teams and other major conference teams his players had to demonstrate great personal commitment to the team and the game of football.

The school administrators and the alumni made it very clear to Jim that they wanted their team to get national recognition—in the form of national television. That translated to big bucks. And, they wanted to hear the victory bell ring. Ringing the bell to celebrate victory was a tradition that began in 1902 after the WSU women's basketball team beat the Washington Huskies. Later, after a football win, members of the Intercollegiate Knights rang the bell in celebration. The tradition continued with the bell being rung by the Student Alumni Connection after each football win. And, the bell only rings in the keys 'G' and 'C', a musical chorus that translates to "Go Cougs!"

"Seen any of the guys yet?" the coach inquired.

"No sir. I wanted to see you first," Rod answered.

Coach turned and grabbed his phone, dialing an extension number. "Harold. Come in here will you? I got someone here that you want to see."

Jim hung up. "He'll be right here. So, you look great."

"I'm feeling good. I'm back up to one seventy-two."

"How's your neck?" Coach asked this with some concern.

"It's fine. The bullet's still in there. The doctors in Spokane didn't think they should try to remove it."

"Well, you'll have to get a clearance from the school's doctor before we can start you. That's for you as much as it is for us."

"Sure coach." Rod hesitated for a breath and then asked, "How about my scholarship, Coach? I'm really gonna need it. I got myself married and my wife's enrolled here now."

"Congratulations, Rod. That's exciting."

Harold Wheeler, the defensive back coach walked in. He stopped and sized Rod up, a big grin on his face.

"I knew a shit-kicker like you would be back. What took you so long, cowboy?" Harold gave him a big handshake.

"Oh, I was takin' her easy, you know, sittin' on my front porch," Rod said with a sardonic grin.

"Oh yeah. I'll bet," Harold said, wryly.

Jim interjected, "Rod was asking about scholarship. He got himself married and she's a student here now."

Harold nodded. "Well that's good, Rod. Maybe she can keep you out of trouble."

"Oh, you don't have to worry about that Coach."

Harold continued, "Your scholarship is available. But you'll have to walk-on. Same rules. You have to earn your spot. But, first you have to go to the clinic and get a review of your file. They need to clear you to play."

"So I heard," Rod replied glancing to Jim.

Harold continued, "You ought to go down to the locker room. I know the boys would be real happy to see that you're back. Then, go see Dr. Cox at the clinic. I'll let him know you're coming over. After that, you and I need to meet."

"Okay, Coach. I guess I'll see you this afternoon."

Walden added, "Rod, I can't tell you how glad I am to see you back here. Made my day. And you are really going to make Junior happy."

"Can't wait to see him."

Rod was out the door and headed down to the locker rooms. He walked into the locker area riding a cloud of high emotion. Even though he knew a doctor had to say yes, Rod would not allow himself to even consider the slightest chance that an M.D. could nix his return to football. It had been such a long road, somehow he had to believe a negative medical report was not in the cards.

Rod came around the corner and saw Junior pulling his gear out of the locker. The big Samoan did not see Rod approach.

Rod was standing right behind him when he said in his best and lowest cowboy tone, "Tupuola, you staying out of trouble?"

Junior froze when he heard the voice. A grin took over his face as he recognized Rod. Junior spun around.

"Rod! Oh my God. Thank God. You are here. Yes!"

He reached out and grabbed Rod, giving him a big, almost bone crushing hug of enthusiasm.

Rod said, "So brother, how are you?"

"I'm fine. What about you? Everything is okay?"

"I'm ready to play. How's them apples?" Rod asked.

Junior was so happy to hear this news.

"I have to go see Doc Cox and then I'll get started. And, I got a surprise. I got my woman here with me. Got myself married."

"Really!" Junior answered. "I can't wait to meet her."

"You will. But listen, I'm going to the clinic now. We'll get together later."

Junior hugged Rod again. He was almost in tears he was so happy to see his old friend.

Dr. Cox had received a call from Harold Wheeler and Jim Walden. He sat with Rod and interviewed him about his general condition. He took Rod through a general examination establishing the current state of blood pressure, heart rate, lung capacity, muscle strength, mobility, balance, and then endurance. Rod flew through the tests. Then the doctor ordered x-rays taken of his neck. The doctor studied the photos and could clearly see the mass in between C-4 and C-5. He had Rod do some extensive head swivel turns and lateral tilts. The doctor checked Rod's muscle strength in his neck, using resistance as a means of measuring strength. After two hours he had Rod meet him in his office.

Rod was ushered to a chair that faced the doctor's desk. While he waited for the doctor to enter he was wondering about the odds of the doctor coming in and saying, "You can't do it. The school cannot take the chance of you injuring yourself while playing. That bullet could shift. If that happens its over."

The five minutes he waited for the doctor seemed like five hours. He thought about the worst things that could happen. Then he thought about what he had survived and overcome of life's scattering of character building circumstances that continued to challenge him. To this day he had not allowed any of it to cause defeat. Yes, in those years after Rick's death he had given up a lot of days to a mental cloud induced by marijuana. Had his mom not pushed him, if he did not have the core character that finally reached up and grabbed hold of his mind, he might have missed out on all that was coming.

Rod had known a few men who had caved in—life's pressures nearly killing them. They had become alcoholics, men who could not face a moment during any day without having braced themselves with liquor. But for the grace of God, Rod could have reached a point as many do, where life could not unfold on any day without the crutch marijuana offered. When hauling trash for his dad's company in the mid to late '70s, two men that the Retherford Sanitation Company gave occasional work to were examples of this condition and Rod worked with them enough to have learned what the old term "rummy" meant. One of the men was a veteran of WWII and had seen one too many a dead body. This man never was able to re-enter civilian life. The other man was an American Indian who had suffered from prejudice—a state of existence prevalent in his younger years. Off the reservation this man, like so many of his brothers, could not find a way to approach life without alcohol.

Walking through life's path on any given day, a step off a curb into a crosswalk one second too soon and a car kills that pedestrian. Rod seemed to understand that decisions made moment-to-moment can change everything. Another day of waking up to a bong load and Rod might never have been able to come out from the haze. At some point lines that are progressing on parallel tracks can intersect and become one. Who knows when the force of one line becomes greater than the force of the other? For Rod, he had a family that cared. And, in this moment he was thinking about the strength of his mother who bargained with him to save his life.

Dr. Cox walked in the office and went directly to his chair. He set Rod's file on the desk and looked over to him.

"Well Rod, you are a bit of a mystery. Take a look at this." The doctor held up one of the x-ray slides and pointed to a white ball adjacent to the neck vertebrae.

Rod studied the photo as the doctor spoke. "Your body's defenses have built a cocoon around the bullet. I am sure that the encasing is hard, calcified probably, and now a permanent part of your neck. The bullet is not going to move."

Rod looked up at him, certainly relieved to here that piece of information.

The doctor continued, "So, I am very pleased to say, yes, you may play football. However, on a note of strong advice, you need to keep the muscle development in your neck a top priority. Protect your vertebrae or you could spend the rest of your life in a chair on wheels. Get my drift?"

Rod had stopped listening the moment he heard, "Yes." That three-letter word made everything that went before completely irrelevant. As he had said to the coach earlier in the day, "I'm back."

Rod sat down that afternoon with Harold Wheeler in the coach's office.

The coach began. "Rod, you are a good old cowboy. You are tough as nails. You have good speed, you hit hard, and you don't show off. When you were with us last year I really liked your curiosity, your willingness to ask questions. You have the talent, but you have to develop your knowledge. I'm giving you the playbook. Study it like you are expecting to be tested on it. We expect you to learn all of it."

So far, Rod had managed to shield his lack of knowledge of offensive strategies. Now he was realizing that to play defense at this level of collegiate sports he needed to know the offense as if he was a running back or receiver. To be effective as a member of this PAC 10 defensive squad, to face the challenge of teams coached by greats like Bill Walsh, John Robinson, Terry Donahue, Roger Theder, and Don James, and most importantly, to not fail Coach Walden or his team, Rod would have to become as mentally skilled as he was physically.

Rod's biggest concern in this moment—with all that he had to learn—was that he needed to ask questions, but to whom? He could not chance revealing this weakness in his knowledge base. This was something that never had surfaced nor mattered until now. In junior college play his physical skill, strength, speed, manner of tackling, and fierce competitive nature was what made him a starter. That was no longer enough.

During the day Patti signed up for the women's volleyball team, and then found her way to the local market, picked up a few groceries and gladly returned to the apartment so she could close out the bustle of the campus. That evening she and Rod had their first home cooked meal in their new apartment. After she gave him the news he wanted to hear, that she was signed up for the team, he recounted his day for her, giving her a blow by blow. He put her to sleep talking through what he was learning about the offensive strategies.

Rod took a short walk after Patti fell asleep. He was so wired with his enthusiasm to play ball, and with all the study he had started on formations, his mind was racing. He could barely wait for the following day when he would suit up and hit the practice field.

He walked over to see Butch, and then the stadium at night. He walked out onto the turf, right to midfield. As he looked around the empty stadium he could hear the crowd noise developing in his thoughts. Rod had yet to experience a game there, but his imagination had played out the experience many a day. After a few moments he walked back towards the apartment. Along the way he had a conversation with his own Butch. He wanted Rick to enjoy every step of this journey. Rick had come this distance with his brother and Rod was certain that without him things would not be the same.

21.

Rod was the first man in the locker room. He could not wait to put on the Cougar uniform and his jersey with his number, 19. As the players returning from the 1980 season came in, Rod was warmly welcomed.

Mike Walker's big smile revealed that silver tooth of his, then he wrapped his arms around Rod giving his old roommate a lift off the floor. "My man, Rod. 'Bout time you showed—brought your white ass back here. How you doin'?"

"I'm doin' great, bro. Doin' great."

Rod's warm greetings continued. Hi-fives and hugs gave way to the ebb and flow of another day—the players mostly treating him as if he was returning from a long weekend. Rod was re-entering the practice routine with a surge of adrenaline such that he felt not a day was missed and the events that unfolded during early September of 1980 were ancient history.

The team hit the practice field and began a warm up routine.

Then the offensive/ defensive drills began. Rod was as fast as ever and he felt complete confidence. As he played, it was evident that Coach Wheeler was keeping an eye on him. Despite the medical clearance it remained a mystery to many that Rod was on that field, making all those moves, putting his body through the stress, the contact, the extreme effort, and with a bullet in his neck.

In a scrimmage that afternoon Rod was covering a receiver man-to-man. The pass was a forty-yard bullet from Mark Rypien, who later would become a Super Bowl MVP with the Washington Redskins. Rod timed it perfectly and got to the ball mid air, catching it. The receiver tangled with him as their feet came back to the turf and the two players fell, Rod slamming down hard on his right shoulder and head. He got up, still cradling the ball. Knowing that he had not lost the timing and could make the physical effort put a big grin on his face. Coach Wheeler could see this, even through the face guard on the helmet. "Looking good, Rod," the coach commented.

As Rod returned to his position, though, he had a sudden sharp pain in his chest that almost dropped him to his knees. His right lung felt as if someone had reached inside his chest cavity, put a vice on his lung, and tightened it. It took his breath. He wanted to wince from the pain but dared not show any sign of any discomfort. He turned ninety degrees from the coach's view and leaned to his side, as if stretching. He was trying to relieve the pain. Within ten seconds the feeling was gone. However, a half-hour later he had the same sensation. Once again, ten seconds passed and the pain subsided.

Later, in the locker room as he was striping off the sweaty practice uniform, Coach Wheeler walked by. "How you feeling, Rod?" he asked.

"I'm good, coach."

"You're shoulder looks pretty hot. Does it feel strange to you?"

Rod looked down and compared left to right. The left shoulder looked normal while the right was reddish-pink, showing a lot of heat. Rod touched it and then said, "Well coach, it's a little warm to the touch. But that's about it."

The coach nodded. "Okay. Get moving. We've got a defensive back meeting in twenty meetings."

As Rod showered the water was soothing. However, when he was drying off he felt a new sensation. As he would touch the right shoulder with the towel he would feel tingles, like the nerves were asleep. The sensation was the same as he had felt many times when leg circulation was cut off from sitting too long. He had no time to dwell on the sensation and pushed on for the defensive back meeting.

Coach Wheeler was reeling through offensive sets, defensive plays, drawing Xs and Os all over the chalkboard so fast that Rod was not following him too well. Terms in football vernacular were in every sentence. Finally, after hearing *Pro Set* several times and not knowing what it meant, Rod was feeling some serious anxiety. Sitting next to him was free safety, Paul Sorenson, fondly referred to by Coach Walden as a "one-man wrecking crew."

Rod turned to Paul in a low voice and asked, "Hey Paul, what's a pro set?"

Paul's response was quick, "Shut up dude. You're gonna get us in trouble."

Rod kept his attention on the coach but continued having trouble following the points to the meeting.

In the hallway after the meeting Rod tried Paul one more time. "Hey Paul, what's a pro set?"

This time Paul could only imagine that Rod was joking. He laughed at the question, shook his head and walked off.

Rod was really concerned, but the question was who to trust. Then he saw Mark Blocker, a player he had bonded with in spring training the year before. Mark had been recruited from junior college and was a scholarship athlete. They had become friends on the first day of practice, Rod's first day at WSU. Being a walk-on Rod was not given any special gear. And, not realizing that he would be playing on Astro Turf he had no shoes for it. Rod was waiting his turn to be timed running forties, the forty-yard dash, when Mark saw his high-top tennis shoes.

Mark walked up to Rod and asked, "Hey dude. Where's your turf shoes?"

Rod quickly covered the truth, not wanting to reveal that he was a walk-on. "Oh, the equipment manager didn't have my size so he's ordered some for me."

Mark responded. "Well that's no good. You can't be running the forties in those. Take mine. I've already had my run." Mark sat down, pulled off his shoes and handed them to Rod.

"Thanks, man. I really appreciate that." Rod put on those shoes and ran his forty. That spontaneous act by Mark would never be forgotten.

When Rod cautiously disclosed to Mark his dilemma of not understanding pro set, Mark took the time to fill Rod in and give him help with his questions.

Over time Rod was to learn the following about the *Pro Set*: in football, the pro set, or split-back formation, was traditional, commonly the foundational set used by school and pro teams. In pro set formations the running backs were lined up side-by-side with each back behind a guard or tackle instead of one in front of the other as in I-formation sets. This was derived from the original, three-running back T-formation, with one of the halfbacks in the T becoming a permanent flanker or wide receiver. Most NFL offensive formations were variations of this concept.

The pro-set was particularly popular since quarterbacks had choices—run or pass. The really quick thinking quarterback might read something in the defensive arrangement and know to take the alternate choice. The beauty in this configuration was that either choice could deliver a successful play. This was important since the defense could only guess what type of play the offense was coming at them with. Since the backs were opposite each other, it took the defense longer to read the gap the offense hoped to run the ball through.

Once a run was established, it was the most dangerous formation in football. The real threat of a team running out of the pro-set was that defenses must respect the play-fake or play-run. This pulled the safety to the line and opened up the middle of the field. And, since both backs were in position to spot an outside blitz, the pro-set formation gave a quarterback ample time to find an open receiver.

Rod would also learn about basic alignments. Players on the defensive side of the ball were generally split between the down linemen—tackles, defensive ends or nose guards, and linebackers and defensive backs—safeties or cornerbacks.

His coach explained the basic defensive alignments. The most typical alignments were four down linemen and three linebackers, a 4-3, however alignments with three down linemen and four linebackers, a 3-4, were used by a number of teams.

On plays where the defense expected the offense to pass, emphasis was often placed on the number of defensive backs. When one of the front seven, down linemen and linebackers, was removed in favor of a defensive back, the five defensive backs were described as a "robber" package. When a sixth defensive back was inserted, it was known as a "dime" package.

Then came the basics about pass coverage. When in obvious running situations, the defense had to be able to account for the eligible receivers on offense. There were two general schemes for defending against the pass that Rod learned.

The first was basic man-to-man, where each eligible receiver was covered by a defensive back or a linebacker. Then there was zone, where some players, usually defensive backs or linebackers, were assigned an area on the field to cover.

In most cases, man-to-man coverage was more effective against short passes, while zone coverage was effective against long passes.

The advanced pass coverage was the next area of study for Rod. Giving an identity to the plays was important. For pass coverage most defensive schemes used the term "cover" and assigned a number or name to describe a particular combination of schemes. There were only five eligible pass receivers on a given play. The quarterback was also an eligible receiver but passes to that position were rare.

In man-to-man defense there were at least seven pass defenders in the 3-4 alignment, and some of the pass coverage personnel might either blitz—bust across the line of scrimmage with the down linemen in an attempt to sack the quarterback, provide double coverage on an intended receiver—or help other defensive players with the pass coverage. In zone coverage, all defensive linebackers and backs would have a specific coverage assignment.

For the Cougs, Cover-Zero was man-to-man coverage with no
help from safeties. This would arise in a blitz play with at least five
players crossing the line of scrimmage. Cover-One was man-to-
man coverage when one safety was not assigned a player to cover
and was available to take on deep pass routes. Cover-Two was
zone coverage with the safeties playing deep, each one covering
their half of the field. Cover-Three was zone coverage—however
in this case extra help was expected from a cornerback so that the
deep zone would be broken into three areas of the field. Cover-
Four—zone coverage again when the corners and safeties would
drop into deep coverage, each one taking their respective quarter
of the field as the offensive play began.

Other coverages that Rod learned included bracket and
high-low coverage. Bracket was a double team scheme to take
out a receiver. This broke down to high-low & in-out. High-low
coverage involved one defensive player staying between the line
of scrimmage and the receiver, protecting against short routes, and
another player behind the receiver to protect from deep routes.

Rod was learning a lot about offensive running and passing. He
had to put his mind into his opponent's. He discovered numerous
ways to beat defensive coverage through this training, and in turn
would compensate in his defensive thinking. For example, on an
"in-route" the receiver would make a ninety-degree turn to the
inside of the field and use his speed to separate from the defensive
back. Another option was the "post-route" that involved a turn of
thirty to sixty degrees to the inside. The receiver used his speed to
separate from the defender and the quarterback would deliver the
ball over the "underneath defender" and far enough inside that
the defender protecting against deep pass could not come down
or across the flight path of the ball to deflect or intercept the pass.

Though the difficulty on this pass was much higher, it could be used for big yardage gains. Reading the development of this kind of play was crucial. Deciding to stay on the receiver, never letting him get beyond Rod, was a challenge but Rod had lightening fast acceleration on his side and agility that no one could surpass.

In-out coverage worked with one defender protecting against routes run to the inside and another protecting against routes to the outside. The easiest way to beat the coverage was a simple go-route: the receiver would sprint down the field past the defenders. Any hesitation on the defenders' part to drop their coverage assignment and run with the streaking receiver could be exploited.

Then there was the zone blitz. This was a brilliant bit of defense where a linebacker or defensive back would blitz. A blitz in football, derived from the WWII term describing heavy air raids intending to obliterate a target, was literally designed to bring extra defensive force across the line of scrimmage to attack the quarterback.

The zone blitz came from Dick LeBeau, and was first evident from 1976 to 1979 when he was with the Green Bay Packers as an assist coach. In college LeBeau had played at Ohio State for the famous Woody Hayes and was on their 1957 national championship team playing at cornerback and halfback. His entire fourteen-year career in the NFL as a player he was with the Detoit Lions, as a defensive back.

Rod was to hear over and over again that effective defense depended on co-operation from defensive players and an understanding of what coverage they were in. That understanding would only happen through lots of study. He was to learn that mixing up defensive alignments and not being predictable was critical. If an offense recognized an alignment or coverage scheme, or the pattern that predicted the use such a scheme, that defensive squad would be taken advantage of by a smart quarterback. And Rod was to face some greats, John Elway at Stanford being one, Jim McMahon at Brigham Young being another.

Then there were special cases that Rod had to factor into his thinking. Players were strong and fast. Rod had speed, he had strength, he had raw determination and virtually no fear. Since he was smaller than most of the players on the field, but hit as hard as anyone, he was a surprise element. His coaches knew to fully exploit every aspect of their player's capabilities. Defensive coordinators looked to players like Rod, with his special skills, in order to surprise the offense.

Rod decided not to disclose the pain he was feeling in his lung to Patti. He called home and told Jim and Chris about the pain, the way his skin was feeling. But in doing this Rod made it clear that he really did not think it would stop him from playing. His dad and Chris agreed that really only Rod would know. They also felt he should not say anything to the coaches for that could cause them to either bench him, or worse, drop him.

Away from the practice field and classrooms Rod always found time for a little half-court basketball. It was a different kind of athletic skill but as importantly, it was a social experience in that he would have the fun of competing with his buddies from the football team in an entirely different discipline. And, being under six feet, Rod was not expected to be able to dunk. He was fast and he was nimble, and on one of those days reminiscent of so many hours he had spent with Andy Mosby playing half-court games, Rod went against Junior Tupuola. As it should happen, Coach Wheeler happened to be walking by and witnessed Rod make a move on Junior during this three on three game. Rod pump faked a pass to the left and Junior bit, moving in the wrong direction. Rod had him and put the ball down, took three steps in, went up and did a one-hand dunk.

Coach Wheeler stopped the game and asked, "Hey Rod, can you do a two hand dunk?"

"Sure," he replied.

"Lets see it."

And Rod turned around and did just that.

He turned around to see Coach Wheeler laughing to himself as he walked away. Later that afternoon as Rod was doing a hurdler's stretch before practice Wheeler came over to him, squatted beside him and said, "I want you to go out and start learning corner."

Rod never played safety again. As the weeks of spring training continued Rod found himself playing right corner, Mark playing left corner. They had a lot of respect for each other's skills. All the studying Rod was doing, and the tutoring that Mark gave him during those early days, really made the difference.

Patti was less than pleased with the dedication and focus required of Rod. Had they been closer to home it might have been easier for her. The school environment, thousands of students and an energy that she was not accustomed to was very intimidating. Patti made it on the volleyball team, but by February had discovered that she was pregnant. The morning sickness began immediately making it nearly impossible for her to play. For Rod, it was a proud moment when she disclosed her condition, but it was short lived since she miscarried. But she immediately was pregnant again, and this child she would carry to full term.

When Rod realized that he was really going to be a father it was a great day. "I'm pregnant again," she announced.

Rod was frozen on the words. "For real?"

Patti smiled. "Yes. This feels right, the first time I knew something was wrong."

"Wow. We've been talking about having a family. To suddenly know that it's happening, wow." He gave her a big hug. Then he thoughtfully added, "You better quit the volleyball team."

"Already did. With the morning sickness I couldn't do it." She took another moment and then added, "I'm going too drop school too after this semester. Rod, I just wanna be a mom."

"Well, okay hun." He was wanting to be supportive and having never been through this he really did not know what to think about Patti's decisions. "So, when is the baby due?"

"December," she answered.

"We'll be a family by the time we have our first anniversary. Think about that."

Patti shifted subjects. "We got word today that HUD approved us for the apartment. We can move in any time."

This was great news for Rod. This meant that once he qualified for a scholarship all his costs were covered.

"Good timing. That means we have a bedroom. You can get started preparing for the baby. You tell you folks yet?"

She smiled. "No. Thought we could call them together."

"Well, lets do that. This is big news. Rod Retherford's gonna have a kid."

That evening the Wright and Retherford clans in the John Day Valley had something to celebrate.

The new apartment was located atop the campus in a complex called North Campus Heights. Rod named the pea gravel stucco buildings Beadrock because it so reminded him of the fantasy town of that name from the motion picture and earlier animated television series, *The Flintstones*.

The Retherford's made fast friends with their neighbors, Tom and Gwen. At that time the young couple were students, each carrying full academic loads. They had a two-year-old boy, Jeremiah. Patti felt an immediate maternal connection to the toddler and wanted to learn as much as she could about child rearing from Gwen.

As no surprise, at the conclusion of spring training Rod had again qualified for his scholarship when he made it to the top of the depth chart. Come fall, it looked like he would play special teams.

Before school broke for summer, Coach Walden spoke to sports reporters at a press conference organized by Rod Commons, the head of media for Washington State University. The purpose of the conference: discuss the upcoming football season and whether the Cougars were going to break a long streak as a team of no promise.

The coach gave the press a lot of enthusiasm in his expectations for the upcoming season. His words were mostly met with a wait-and-see attitude. The following day Walden was quoted in the newspapers speaking about Rod: "Rod came back to us as a walk-on and was impressive in drills this spring. He finished spring ball second on the depth chart at right corner. And, he looks a good bet for special teams duty, too. I was pleasantly surprised by him when he came up here last fall. Now, he's a twenty-three year-old junior who has shown us he is willing to learn. He will be a torpedo on special teams. You know, Rod's ridden those wild Brahma bulls and playing football is, well, it's a step down when it comes to rough and tough action for him. He's intense and has the physical ability to play."

After the press conference Rod Commons fielded questions about Rod from a couple of aggressive reporters.

One asked, "Isn't this the player that was shot last fall?"

The other one demanded, "We want to talk to him."

"Rod's gone home for the summer, boys. You will meet him in the fall."

The truth, as media head Commons knew, was that Rod needed to be prepared for the onslaught of curiosity. He was news-worthy, but needed preparation.

Before the accident Rod Commons had met Rod Retherford briefly. When the accident occurred Commons felt the prevailing attitude about Rod was that Washington State University had seen the last of him on a football field. Everyone in the media department and others he spoke to around campus only hoped that Rod would return to WSU as a student, finish his education, and have a decent life.

So when Jim Walden called Rod Commons and said, "Rod Retherford's coming back!" the coach heard only silence.

Commons finally replied, "You gotta be kiddin' me?"

"I'm dead serious, son. We're talking about a cowboy here."

Commons knew well what that term meant. He had grown up in Oregon on a ranch. Rod Retherford was not the dime store variety, he was the real deal.

"We're going to have quite a story to play out with this. I mean, you talk about inspiration? Hell, even the papers in Seattle, LA, and the bay area will want this story," Commons added.

Walden, being a smart fellow himself added, "And it will probably help us with the national TV boys. We want the Cougars on ABC." He laughed, "Won't have to convince Keith Jackson, though."

"That's for sure." Commons said.

Rod and Patti were able to hold onto their apartment during summer even though they returned to John Day. The summer was a quick one. He worked as a lifeguard for those eight weeks and that gave him an opportunity to workout as a part of his job. He would begin the workday with a series of ten timed two hundred meter sprints, clocking at twenty-seven seconds. He also kept up his weight lifting regimen. Meanwhile Patti was past morning sickness and was enjoying the experience of carrying her first child.

Fall training arrived in a heartbeat, not one moment too soon for Rod. The couple returned to Pullman and settled into Bedrock again. Tom and Gwen were happy to have them back as neighbors, and the little one seemed to be happy to see them as well. After a few weeks Patti announced to Rod, "I'm going to sit Jeremiah for Tom and Gwen. I'll make a little food money for us, and help them out with their school load. Maybe I can take in a few others."

Rod was pleased. It would help out with their extremely tight budget, but just as important, this responsibility would gave Patti something to fill out her days. Rod knew her days were long, his time being totally absorbed with football practice and study on top of the academic load of a full time student.

As the season opener approached Rod was, as Walden had said, a torpedo on special teams. Joe Albi Stadium, an outdoor multi-purpose athletic stadium in Spokane, hosted some of the Washington State Cougar games since so many of their alumni were located in that area. The stadium was packed for the Cougs first game as they faced Montana State. This was Rod Retherford's first game for a PAC 10 school, though Montana was a non-conference game. The Cougs showed their stuff and the fans got an early sense of what promise this team held for the unfolding season. Rod recorded two tackles and three assists, playing a very solid game. The headline in the paper read, "Cougars do the Job, Blitz Montana State 33 to 21." To make this even sweeter for Rod, the newspaper carrying that headline had a photograph of Rod during a kickoff as his speed propelled him into the Montana State offensive wedge. What none of them knew was Rod's right lung feeling the vice grip of pain was a constant issue. During plays it had not taken his breath away, yet. But he had a number of times while waiting for the offensive huddle to break where he used his all to contain the pain.

Journalist Sue Manning interviewed Rod after the game. Her next edition story's title was "Bullet in the neck was a shot in the arm." A photograph of Rod sporting his number 19 jersey accompanied the story and it was picked up by the Associated Press. The focus of the story was on Rod's amazing recovery from the accident. For Rod, this was a little taste of the press and their growing interest in him.

Before the next game Rod Commons took a few minutes with Rod who, while happy to see stories about his life in print, was concerned that the writers were only interested in the accident.

Rod Commons shook his head. "You know Rod, you make for great press. Your story is simply inspirational. It's not too many times these writers get to reach into the human drama side of reporting on games. It's usually recapping plays, talking about records, or occasionally writing about an injury on the field. In your case, its like you're a walking miracle. So, you need to brace yourself. You're going to be asked the same five questions over and over and over. It's just the way it is."

Rod answered, "But I'm a football player. Aren't they interested in that too?"

"Frankly, not as much as how you managed to be one today," Commons said. He just looked at the young player after that. Rod began to nod, expressing his understanding of what he would certainly face.

This was sound advice and prediction from Rod Commons. It was so very true that blood, sex, and crime stories were exciting reading and would carry people away from the routines of their life. And, that was what sold newspapers. For the celebrity of the world, whether sports, entertainment, or political, being in the limelight at whatever level was a price that came with the glory. Some handled it well, some believed their own press, some shied from it. Fortunately, Rod had a support mechanism in the Washington State Media department. Rod also was smart. He managed to get writers to pay attention to his game, but always giving them enough about the accident to juice up their story.

The WSU campus was buzzing with excitement after defeating Montana St. Parties were happening everywhere and needless to say, the football players were heroes. For the handful of guys that were married, those great parties were not in their social routine. And, for Rod with Patti pregnant, his after game routine would take him directly home.

To leave all the excitement behind and return to the pressure of domestic life was something normally reserved for a time well after college years. Rod's resolve to have a family weighed in here and he considered the tradeoff of married domestic life to be a part of his responsibility as a husband, period. While his buddies were going off to conquer the night he would find himself doing a brief recap of the game with Patti over a simple dinner. They had no spare money ever, for any kind of celebration. Certainly, it was hard for Rod to come off the high of the game, but he realized it would be equally hard for her to go through the great detail of it that would have happened if he were hanging out with his teammates.

Patti attended the home games and those within driving range of Pullman. For the drive-to games, the traditional parties were something that the players really had fun with. But again, Rod and the other married players would return to their motel rooms and a domestic evening with their spouses.

The 1981 season began shaping up with the Cougars rising to national attention. Their second game was at Colorado. This being Rod's first distant away game, he had the experience of jet travel across the Rockies to Denver. The University of Colorado, at that point one hundred and five years old, was located north west of Denver in Boulder. As were all the athletes, Rod was walking tall wearing his official Cougar polo shirt and traveling as a PAC 10 athlete boarding the flight.

The game was a close one for the Cougars. The WSU offensive game was not working, and Walden was later to take the responsibility for his poor game plan. He was also to strongly compliment the defensive squad for holding the score within reach for the hapless offense. With four minutes left in the game the Cougs were down only 10-0 to the Colorado Buffaloes. The Cougs forced them into a punt situation at the Buffalo forty-yard line. Walden called for his team to try for a block on the punt. Jeff Keller, a receiver on the punt return team, busted through and got his hand out in time to block the punt. The ball took a Cougar friendly hop right into the one-man wrecking crew, Paul Sorenson, who took off on a fifty yard run that put six points on the board. They made the field goal and with close to four minutes left on the clock the Cougs were suddenly in the game, only down by three.

Once again the defense stopped the Buffaloes near midfield. And, to the great surprise of the Cougar coaches, they again broke through the line. The Cougar defenders put such a rush on the Colorado punter he knew he would never get the ball off his foot in time. He tucked the ball in his arms and was tackled.

With a little over a minute of play left Cougar quarterback Ricky Turner drove his team to a first and goal. A badly timed handoff almost turned to a disaster, but once again a Cougar friendly bounce put Ricky in motion and he ran in for a touchdown.

Ricky was a highly sought after prospect that Arizona State, among others, tried to recruit. But they wanted him as a wide receiver. Walden wanted Ricky, but as a quarterback. The young man from Compton, California, had great film on his elusive and lightening fast moves. WSU only succeeded in signing Ricky when Coach Walden flew to Los Angeles, sat down with Ricky's grandmother, looked her in the eyes and promised that the young man would have the opportunity to play as the quarterback and fulfill his longtime dream. Fortunately, the Cougars had a head coach who spoke with his eyes as much as with his friendly Mississippi-bred voice, and it all rang true to the loving grandmother. She told Ricky to sign with Washington State.

The Cougs defeated the Buffaloes 14-10. It was this game that not only convinced Coach Walden that Washington State University was on their way to a great season, but it spoke loudly to every member of the team. The Cougs were coming into their own. Lookout PAC 10.

Their remarkable season continued on a roll with an at home, Martin Stadium, on campus win against Arizona State, 24-21, another at home win against Pacific, 31-0, and their fifth straight win of the season at Oregon State University in Corvallis, 23-0. The first halt in that remarkable momentum came in their home game against UCLA that ended in at 17-17 tie in front of 40,000 WSU emotionally exhausted fans. Included in those numbers were Rod's family and Uncle Tats.

The next game for Washington State was in Tucson, at the University of Arizona. Rod was the kicking team wedge breaker. He was given this roll for two reasons. He was a fierce heads up tackler, and he had great acceleration. The wedge breaker would stand about eight yards further back then the rest of the team when they lined up for the kick off. It was for Rod to time his accelerating sprint so that as the ball was kicked he would blow past his teammates and accelerate directly at the protective wedge that the kick return specialist would follow. For Rod, these three or four men were bowling pins that he wanted to strike.

The Cougars kicked to open the game. True to form Rod accelerated and went straight at the wedge. This was a one hundred seventy-two pounder going head on into a wedge of two hundred thirty pound linebackers. The linebackers braced up for the contact and indeed Rod took two of them out, but being as light as he was, he went two feet in the air on contact with four hundred sixty pounds of players accelerating at him. Spinning and drifting to his left from the energy of the hit Rod managed to land on his feet aimed towards the left corner of the Arizona end zone. He was near the sidelines and had a perfect line on Vance Johnson, the Wildcats kick returner, who was just coming around the corner and planning to sprint up-field towards the sideline. Rod nailed Vance head on, right on the chest, wrapping his arms around the runner, picking him up and taking him back about four yards.

The Wildcats fell to the Cougars 34-19. Rod was a big part of the enormous defensive effort. As a wedge breaker six times during that game he made tackles on five of those six plays.

The following week the Cougs traveled to Southern California to face the Trojans and none other than Marcus Allan. Allen had one of the most spectacular seasons in NCAA history going for him that year. To put this into perspective, by the season's end he would have rushed for 2,342 yards, and would become the first player in NCAA history to rush for over 2,000 yards in one season. He also would gain a total of 2,683 offensive yards. He would lead the nation in scoring, and would win the Heisman Trophy, the

Maxwell Award, and the Walter Camp Award. He was also named the PAC 10 Player of the Year.

Jim Walden knew his kids were up against a true dynasty. Not only did USC have a wealth of talent, they had wealth behind them. They played in the enormous 92,516 seat Los Angeles Memorial Coliseum, a structure built in the early 1920s. It's first football game dated June 6, 1923. The coliseum had played host to one Olympiad and the second was scheduled for 1984. It had been the venue for the 1967 and 1973 Super Bowls, and the 1959 World Series. It had been home to the Trojans it's entire existence, and was home to the Los Angeles Rams, plus the expansion home of the San Diego Chargers in 1960, and the Los Angeles Raiders were headed there the following year, 1982.

When the Cougars arrived at the stadium, to say most of them were awe struck would be an enormous understatement. This was Jim Walden's second trip to the coliseum. The Cougs 1979 team had lost to the Number 1 ranked and defending national champion Trojans on this same field.

For Rod it was a surreal experience to be standing on the field with such history, the place of so many games he had seen on his parent's television, long before the thought had occurred to him that he could play PAC 10 football. As the opening ceremony was taking place and teams were being introduced he leaned over to Bill Gribble, a corner and punt returner, and said, "Do you believe we are standing here? We are about to play USC. It doesn't get any better than this."

A few moments later the Trojan mascot, the white horse named Traveler, approached with a Trojan warrior in the saddle dressed in full regalia, his sword drawn and about to begin a galloping charge. Just as the ritual was about to begin, the rider was thrown when Traveler was spooked—bucking his rider off his back.

Rod being a longtime cowboy and rodeo competitor, had a tradition well set in his bones. Having seen many a rodeo parade as had all the hardcore competitors, he would love it when one of the dudes dressed in fancy gear riding in the pre-show would be bucked off a horse. And this moment, as the Trojan landed on his ass was no exception. To most others it was an accident in which they held their breath hoping for no injury. For Rod, this was a fall down with laughter moment.

Unfortunately, the balance of the day was not so pleasurable. The Cougars were handed their first loss of the season, 17-41 in front of 61,000 fans. Rod had the great experience of defending against Marcus Allen. In one play he got the initial hit on Allen, and as the game progressed he had several assists.

On Sunday, November 1, they traveled home to Pullman licking their wounds. Jim Walden wasted no time grabbing a-hold of his players minds. "Okay, we got an ass-kicking. We went up against a national powerhouse with our six—one—and oh record, and we were humbled. But think about it. You guys scored seventeen points against the defending national champions. And our defense faced Marcus Allen, who is breaking records and will no doubt be the Heisman winner. The way you grow is to challenge yourself against someone greater. Well, you went up against one of the best. You gave it the best you had. I'm damn proud of you kids. You all gained a huge experience, and—it's in the record books. Now it's time to begin thinking about the University of Oregon next Saturday. That's the only game that matters, not what just passed at USC. The Cougars fate is back in your hands."

Patti was one month away from the baby's due date. Rod was glad to be home since the magic time was so close. The balance of his season was within Washington State, so if she went into labor early, Rod would be within reach. The pregnancy had been very normal. Patti was a healthy young woman and the doctors had no reason to suspect any problems. So neither expecting parent had any concerns, they just wanted to be within a reasonable distance of each other.

The University of Oregon game was held at home in Pullman. It was a major victory for the Cougars and they pounded Oregon 39-7 and continued on a road towards a possible bowl bid. There were a few major obstacles to overcome and Cal was one of them. But what arrived with that game was a hand dealt by mother nature in the form of gale force winds blowing right down the Joe Albi Stadium field in Spokane, creating an equal amount of havoc for each team. Roger Theder, Cal's coach was quoted after the game saying "That was the most unusual football game I've been associated with."

What Theder was covering in those words was not just the monsoon conditions that prevailed during much of the game, but he was also referring to Cal only making 99 net yards against what was described as a "varied and swarming WSU defense." The death blow was dealt to Cal at 13:31 on the clock in the fourth quarter when the Cougs punted from behind their 25-yardline. The ball hit Cal's Kevin Moen's foot and Rod Retherford was in the right place at the right time, making a crucial and ultimately game winning recovery. This play turned the tide and fully deflated Cal. The Cougs went on and won 19-0.

To the Cougars delight and surprise, their archrivals, the University of Washington Huskies defeated the University of Southern California Trojans in an unexpected win, knocking Southern Cal out of the Rose Bowl race and placing WSU one step closer to their first bowl game in fifty years.

Their list of conquests in that memorable season put them at the top of the PAC 10 and headed in the direction of Pasadena on New Years Day. All they had to do was knock off the University of Washington Huskies at Seattle in the annual Pacific Northwest event, the Apple Cup. This year that meant playing in Husky Stadium. No one but Coach Walden could appreciate what playing in Husky Stadium meant. While the L.A. Coliseum was huge, Husky stadium would be packed with the Cougars' nemesis. This was a game of legend as others in the country, such as Notre Dame verses USC or Army verses Navy. Those two rivalries were comparable to the fever that set in with the anticipation each year of the final conference game for these two Washington State teams.

Husky Stadium is an outdoor athletic stadium on the campus of the University of Washington in Seattle. The stadium's U-shaped design was specifically oriented (18.167° south of due east) to minimize glare from the sun in the athletes' eyes. The open end overlooks scenic Lake Washington and the Cascade Mountains.

Only four Division I-A stadiums are older: Georgia Tech's Bobby Dodd, 1913; Mississippi State's Scott Field, 1915; Cincinnati's Nippert, 1916; and Wisconsin's Camp Randall, 1917. Husky stadium was one of thirty-four structures built before the 1929 stock market crash.

Husky Stadium was one of only two schools that has some fans traveling to the football games by boat. There have been upwards of 12,000 more people out on Lake Washington next to Husky Stadium, some of whom spend the entire weekend aboard their boats celebrating the rivalry.

Because of the size and design of Husky Stadium, close to seventy percent of the seats are located between the end zones, and it is considered one of the top ten college football stadiums in the nation. At times the sound level makes it nearly impossible to think, getting so loud that it could cause pain because anyone within the area of the stadium could literally feel the noise. During televised games, it sometimes got so loud that the camera vibration would be visible on TV. In later years ESPN measured the crowd noise at 135 decibels, well above the threshold of pain.

Jim Walden had been there and knew every bit of this history. He knew that his kids were about to face the game of their season, for some it would be the game of their life. Win this and they were in the Rose Bowl. Washington State had a history in the historic annual Pasadena event. In 1916 they defeated Brown 14-0 in the first annual Rose Bowl. They played Alabama in the Rosebowl in 1931 and lost 24-0.

The Apple Cup was a tradition that began in 1900. This game was to be the seventy-fourth meeting of these two schools. Jim Walden as head coach, had succeeded in bringing victory and national athletic prominence back to Pullman, Washington, after many years of silence. The pressure he felt for his boys was extreme, but it was his intent to not allow them to buy into it. If they would manage to be themselves, play at the top of their game, they could defeat the Huskies.

The Cougs were entering this game at the top of the PAC 10 with five wins, one tie, and one loss. Their overall record was eight wins, one tie, and one loss. A Washington State victory would put the Cougars in the Rose Bowl regardless of what UCLA did because the Cougs overall record gave them one more win than UCLA. This was a huge accomplishment in itself, and generally there's nothing as sweet as an Apple Cup victory, whether a bowl game is the prize or not. This year, it having been fifty years since a Cougar team was in the Rose Bowl, Walden and his kids were going for the whole shooting match.

The game got off to a start with Mother Nature once again playing a factor. Through the first half and up eight seconds prior to halftime, the Cougs were leading 7-3. It was raining and the turf was slippery. The Husky quarterback, Steve Pelluer, uncorked a pass right in the corner of the end zone to receiver Paul Skansi. Cougar defender, Nate Bradley, was in perfect position to pick off the pass. Just as he went for the reception his feet gave way to the soggy turf and instead of intercepting the ball he went face first into the mud. Skansi made the catch and the Cougs went into the locker room down 10-7. Momentum turned on that play. This circumstance was compounded when Cougar quarterback, Clete Casper, suffered a pulled hamstring not long before the half. Though the Cougs had Ricky Turner to bring in, he was not experienced enough to deal with the noise level and emotion of the fans. The Cougs ultimately went down to the Huskies 23-10.

The Huskies managed to knock the Cougars out of the Rose Bowl in 1981's Apple Cup. The saving grace, the team got word that they were invited to play in the Holiday Bowl in San Diego. This would be their first bowl game in fifty years. This was big news. On the team bus, despite the pain of the Apple Cup loss, Rod was feeling the joy of his team making it into a bowl game. He could not understand why no one was talking about what that meant.

He finally went to Coach Walden and asked, "Hey coach, I know the Rose Bowl is the big granddaddy and all, and yes, it's a real bummer to have lost to the Huskies. But, how about this team showing some excitement and pleasure around the Holiday Bowl invitation? We're playing a major post season, nationally televised game. I'm really excited. Am I nuts?"

Coach Walden looked at him nodding. "No. You're not nuts

Rod. You are very right. And, I'm very proud that we have brought the first bowl game in half a century to Washington State."

The coach went on to light a fire under his kids and bring all this into the right kind of light.

The Apple Cup was November 20, 1981. Rod was back home in time to take Patti to the hospital and be a part of the birth of his first child, Brooke, who was born November 30th. As he held his firstborn child in his arms that last day of November, Rod Retherford had just realized his biggest dream in life, to become a dad. It was the first one of what would eventually be the three proudest moments of his life.

There was another extraordinary aspect of this, and one very personal to Rod. As he cradled his tiny and beautiful daughter he had his first conversation with her away from the ears of anyone. "Brooke, you are going to take your first trip with your dad and mom, all the way down to San Diego in eleven days. You have made us into the Retherford family. That makes your dad here, real happy. And, my little girl, you'll be with your dad when he plays football in the Holiday Bowl. So, you can cheer for my team, whoop it up and let everyone know that you are a Cougar."

Anyone reading these words are likely a football fan, or are perhaps about to become one. The passion that students have for their schools is fairly common. Understanding what it is to be a Cougar is another matter. That university built in the Palouse, by virtue of its location and relationship to the land around it, puts a fierce fire in the belly of all who have attended it. For Rod to share his passion for the game and his school with his infant child was a moment waiting to happen for the twenty-three years of his life. It was the first day instilling tradition as a part of Brooke's young life.

And, indeed, game day, December 18, 1981 arrived in beautiful San Diego. The city, located at the southern tip of Southern California, had a warm climate cooled by the on-shore flow from the Pacific.

Rod was dressed in his uniform and on the field before a pre-game warm up. He cradled his girl in the middle of that stadium, a proud dad gazing at those curious tiny eyes. And he once again had a private conversation with his little girl. "My sweet little one, you hoot and holler for your daddy today. But I want you to know something. You being here is what matters to me. Everything that's happened getting to this day doesn't mean anything anymore. I know you can't understand any of that now, but one day we'll talk about all that stuff. But you have fun with your mom today." He gave her a kiss and handled that most precious bundle of joy back to Patti.

The Cougars were facing Brigham Young University. They had three straight appearances in the Holiday Bowl as champions of the Western Athletic Conference. And they had Jim McMahon at quarterback. That meant they had a passing game that was far more critical to their offense then their running game. The Cougs had a stronger running game on the other hand. In regular season play the match up would have probably swung in favor of the WSU Cougars. But returning from a six-week hiatus it is difficult to get the timing of a running game back.

At halftime the Cougs were getting pounded. Jim Walden looked his kids in the eyes in the locker room. "You guys have had a grand time down here in San Diego. Everything's been first-cabin. Now, if you guys would like to decide to begin playing, well that would be just fine with me. You can beat these guys. And, frankly, I'd like to see you hand McMahon a loss."

McMahon's attitude and rude behavior in the pre-game day schedule of activities was cited in the press. Aboard the U.S.S. *Kitty Hawk*, at a luncheon in honor of both teams, McMahon was bored, and so he put his head on folded arms as if he was sleeping. After the game a reporter asked a defensive lineman, Ken Collins, "Tell us about the Holiday Bowl experience for you guys. What did you think of it?"

Ken responded, "The time we had was wonderful, in fact, the only negative thing about the whole experience is that Jim McMahon was the biggest asshole I've ever seen."

Coach Walden was to later speak with Ken and say, "Next time you're interviewed son, why don't you just tell everyone what you really feel?" However, Walden could not disagree with Ken's characterization of McMahon.

The Cougs came out from the locker room after the halftime break and brought the score back to 38-36. Ultimately that was the final score of the game. Rod had played very well, as did the entire team. He recorded two solo tackles among the many assists. He had a near interception of a McMahon pass on the BYU nine-yard-line when he read the pass and went back, the other way from the intended receiver, but just as he got his hands on the ball he slammed into the ground. The ball came loose and was ruled an incomplete pass.

The 1981 season was over. But Jim Walden's Washington State Cougars had earned the first spot in a bowl in fifty years. This broke down a mental barrier for the teams that were to follow. And when considering that in 1981 there were only a few bowl games compared to later years, this was an accomplishment worth celebrating. The Holiday Bowl game appearance affected recruiting, it put the Cougars on the national radar and began to change that long standing tide that was drawing away from Pullman rather than approaching the campus.

The effect was felt statewide. Washington State Senate Resolution 1981-156 was passed and in part stated the following:

"Whereas, For the first time in forty-five years, the intrastate rivalry between the Huskies and the Cougars decided the Pacific 10 Rose Bowl representative: and . . .

. . . Whereas, The Cougars will be playing in the Holiday Bowl, their first bowl game appearance in fifty-one years; . . .

. . . Whereas, This represents a fundamental and basic shift in the power base of the Pac 10 Conference from Southern California to the State of Washington; . . .

. . . Whereas, The two schools have two of the finest coaches in the nation who emphasize both the development of athletic ability and character amongst their ball players; . . .

. . . Whereas, This is the first time ever that both the Huskies and the Cougars will be appearing in bowl games in the same year;

"NOW, THEREFORE, BE IT RESOLVED, By the Senate of the State of Washington, That even though in a contest of skills of this nature there must be victors and vanquished, both the Huskies and the Cougars and the State of Washington as a whole, stand as winners as a result of this football season; . . ."

When Jim Walden heard the resolution being read a thought passed through his mind. He was the fourth coach in the four seasons prior to 1981. There had been a gaffe he heard from many a cynic about Cougar football that went, "The Martin Stadium scoreboard read "Home," and on the other side instead of "Visitor" it read "Winner". Jim grinned knowing whoever started that clever line was never to repeat it again.

In an interview the coach was asked about the character of the

1981 team as opposed to earlier teams. Jim responded thoughtfully. "You know, as a coach you hear all these theories being floated by the guys who do the Monday Morning Quarterbacking. All the ifs. My daddy used to say, if the dog hadn't stopped to pee, hell, he woulda' caught the rabbit. He was a character in the truest sense of the word. And, he had a lot of character that he passed onto me. It takes a team with character, and it takes the characters of the team in balance to make it all work. I mean, look at us. We got ourselves multi-dimensional, multi-racial, urban and rural character. We got it all on this team. I love these kids and they've been a complete pleasure to coach."

Rod Retherford was a key component in the defensive half of a team that made history in the state of Washington and in the PAC 10 conference in the 1981 season. He and his teammates under the guidance of the entire coaching staff, Jim Walden at the helm, had written new pages for the chronicles of the Palouse.

Rod, the kid that was too-small to play varsity ball in John Day, who was emotionally bankrupt after his brother's death, who gave his mind over to street procured mental sedatives like marijuana and booze, who got his act together thanks to the strong hand and passionate belief of his mother, who then was dropped to the ground, seemingly a quadriplegic in the aftermath of that accidental gun shot and told that he may not survive, who dropped from school out of depression, had fought his way back to rejoin the Cougars against the biggest odds he would ever face, played in this season of seasons for Washington State University.

Rod Retherford earned his place in the Cougar history of the great university located in that beautiful Palouse country.

Rod with Brooke, the Holiday Bowl, 1981

23.

The hoopla of the 1981 season finally subsided, and reality returned, as it always will. Rod had life to face and that meant books, school, and most importantly, raising his daughter. On January 11, 1982, Rod and Patti, with their little girl, celebrated their first wedding anniversary.

In a world where he could have afforded to splurge he would have replayed the dinner they had on their honeymoon night by once again taking Patti to a Chinese restaurant for a dinner out on the town. That had been all they could afford on the night of their wedding. For their first anniversary it was more than these two could afford. They were just making it each month with only a few pennies to spare. And this was not because of any frivolous behavior, it was simply the fact of living on a student scholarship budget and feeding a family of three.

Rod wanted to replicate the honeymoon night. He scraped together the spare coins he could find in the apartment and went to the local market. He searched the food aisles studying prices and found that they could afford a can of Chung King Chow Mein and noodles. He brought this treasure home for their celebration dinner and the two, a proud dad and mom, with their infant daughter as witness, had their first anniversary dinner in their humble apartment.

Rod's senior year, 1982, he was chosen as starting corner playing opposite his friend Mark Blocker who was left corner. The Monday before the first game Rod was suited up and heading for the practice field. Coach Wheeler was standing at the end of the tunnel and stopped Rod as he headed out for practice.

"Rod, come over here. We need to talk," the coach said in a very serious way.

They stepped out of the way of the other players. The coach asked, "Did you go to Oregon State University?"

"Yes. Only for a couple of weeks out of high school, but . . ."

Wheeler cut him off mid sentence. "You can't play here."

Rod was shocked and realized this was serious dialog hitting him between the eyes. "What are you talking about?"

The Coach offered a brief answer. "You attended a Division I school. You have to layout a year if you go to another Division I school. Looks to me like the only school you can play for now is Oregon State. I can give them a call and put in the word for you."

"This can't be happening. I went there for two weeks straight out of high school. I never attended any classes. I withdrew before the deadline and got Ws on all my classes. I stayed in John Day for a couple of years and then went to junior college before walking on here. You know what I've been through. Doesn't any of that count? For Christ's sake coach, I just made it as a starter in a PAC 10 school."

The coach knew that Rod was really upset. This was a disastrous blow to a young man who had worked so hard, brought himself back to school against the greatest odds.

The coach contemplated a thought then asked, "Did you turn out for any sports or accept any equipment at Oregon State?"

Rod answered firmly, "No."

The coach thought for another minute. "All right. Go on out to practice. I'm going to go speak with John Chaplin. I'll see you later."

He wheeled around and walked off. Rod stood there wondering if this was some cruel joke about to played on him. Once again the life had been snatched from him in an instant. Was this to be the story of his life? How could the world he lived in be so cruel?

John Chaplin was not only the head track coach at the university, but he also managed all the athletic eligibility questions. He was the man who might have the answer.

Rod's morning practice was less than spectacular. He felt as if the grim reaper had a hand on his shoulder again. It was later that day that Coach Wheeler walked up to him with a big grin and came right out with, "Looks like you're good to play."

That was the end of the eligibility crisis. Rod looked to the heavens and thanked the Lord and then put his head back in the game.

In the ramp up to that first game the press began a campaign that minimized any expectation for the defense. The season was beginning with Rod, Mark Blocker, Steve Haub and Joe Taylor as first year starters. Before they ever had a chance to play a game the press took issue with their lack of experience.

The first scheduled game was at Joe Albi Stadium and WSU recorded a resounding victory over the University of Idaho, 34-14 in front of 25,321 screaming Cougs.

Entering into Rod's thoughts now was the long shot possibility of going on to the pros after college. He considered the avenues available as he went through the year. A winning season would certainly help him get attention. The continued interest in Rod Retherford, gun shot survivor, kept his name prominent in the press at virtually any town the team played in. The accumulation of stories could only help him get noticed.

In that season opener, however, Rod took due note of the fact that Coach Wheeler was rotating a junior, Tracy Atkins, in for Mark Blocker on one series and then in for Rod on another. This had gone on throughout that first game. The following Monday Rod went to see the Coach.

"Coach I've noticed you rotating Tracy into the corner spots. What's up with that?" Rod asked.

"Well, Tracy grades out at ninety percent on the practice field and ninety percent in the classroom."

Rod wasted no time countering. "Last year I graded out in the nineties and I was never rotated in for Jeff. I played the season as you placed me and never expected anything more. But this year, I believe I've earned my spot, coach. I don't think its fair to be rotated out by a junior when I'm playing as well as I am. If the wheel ain't broke, don't fix it. And I don't have to tell you, you're a coach, this is the PAC 10. Sometimes you just have to wait your turn. Plus, I like to think I may have a chance at the pros. They aren't gonna take notice of me if I'm not the starter playing his own spot exclusively. I might be making a big mistake saying this to you coach, but either play me or play Tracy. I feel that strongly about it."

The coach listened and then said, "I'll think about it and get back to you."

That evening during practice, Rod was not rotated out. The coach never said anything to him, but Wheeler's actions were the answer. Rod played the season at right corner, exclusively.

But the season turned into a major disappointment for one reason: injuries. The greatest talent and preparation means nothing if twenty-two players are out on injury. That is exactly what happened to the Cougars. After their first win they recorded six losses broken by one tie.

Along that path they played Stanford at Martin Stadium, and John Elway was quarterback. He was having an extraordinary season, averaging roughly three hundred fifty yards passing per game. He was ranked number one in the nation. The Cougars came into that game one—five—and one. With just under three minutes left in the game the Cougs were ahead of the Stanford Cardinals 26-24. The defense had held Elway to eighty-five yards passing. Stanford Coach, Paul Wiggin was quoted in the news reports on the game saying, "they [WSU] took away our passing game." By the time this game was over the Cougars had lost most of their starting players of the season to injury. Stanford went on to defeat WSU 31-26. Had the Cougs stayed healthy in 1982 it would have been quite a different outcome. During that game Rod had ten tackles and he kept his man covered so well that Elway only threw at him once.

The next week the Cougars traveled to Eugene, home of the University of Oregon, for their ninth game of the season, on November 6th. For Rod, this was a very personal game because the Autzen Stadium crowd would include many people from John Day that knew Rod but had never seen him play. And, his old friend Steve Baack was playing defensive end for the Ducks.

Coach Walden picked Rod as team captain. Twenty thousand

Oregonians saw home grown Rod Retherford represent his team at the beginning of the game. Those same folks witnessed Rod defending in a bump and run situation. Rod kept the Ducks number 23, Rourke Lowe, shoulder-to-shoulder in a man-to-man run down the sideline for fifty yards. Rod looked over his shoulder at the exact moment the ball came out of quarterback Kevin Lusk's hand. He timed his jump exquisitely and rotated one hundred eighty degrees and hauled in an interception. Lowe reached out and got a handful of Rod's jersey but the pass was Rod's. He ran off the field holding the ball and handed it to the equipment manager, asking, "Hey, put this in an equipment bag for me."

The manager replied, "I can't do that. The officials will want it back."

Rod took the ball back from the manager and walked to Coach Walden. "Coach, don't you think an Oregon boy oughta keep an Oregon ball?"

This was an official 1982 season University of Oregon ball. It was imprinted as such and of course was a memento of great meaning.

Walden got one of his big Mississippi grins and responded, "Sure boy. Throw it in a bag. If they bill us for it, you'll have to pay."

Rod nodded, turned to the equipment manager and tossed him the ball.

The Cougs defeated the Ducks 10-3. This was a proud day for Rod. After the game a high school track buddy of Rod's, Dave Smith, came up to him, grabbed the front of Rod's jersey and walked Rod backwards while saying, "Retherford, you little shit, that was some awesome playing."

Then Rod felt a bear hug that came up from behind him as

Steve Baack, six feet four inches, lifted him off the ground saying, "You're just a stud, aren't you!"

When Steve put Rod down they hugged. Rod said, "It really meant a lot to me to play this game against you, Steve. Just two John Day kids having some fun."

For Rod, this game in front of so many people he had known, was as important a game as any in his two year collegiate career at Washington State.

The following week the Cougars traveled to Berkeley where they racked up their last loss before the arrival of the 1982 Apple Cup. It was the first Apple Cup scheduled in Pullman in twenty-eight seasons, the last game of the season, and the last game for Rod Retherford as a Cougar.

The game was November 20th, ten days before Brooke's first birthday. Martin Stadium was alive with 40,000 fans hungry to see the University of Washington Huskies fall at the hands of the Washington State University Cougars. If the Huskies won the game they were Rose Bowl bound again. The Huskies were nine and one, and had been ranked number one in the nation three times during the season. How could they lose? The Huskies had the likes of Steve Pelluer passing, Paul Skansi receiving, and 1981 Rose Bowl MVP Jacque Robinson, running. They had been in two straight Rose Bowls and arrived in Pullman ranked number three in the country.

As was typical the Cougars came out for their warm up wearing gray pants with the crimson jerseys. Back in the locker room before the game started the coaches went through their last minute comments. The final thing that Coach Walden said, "Change into your Crimson pants before you return to the field."

The players were surprised. This had never happened before.

Walden could read the question in their eyes and added, "Maybe this change will bring you guys some luck."

Having been plagued with injuries all season none of the press writers had considered that some of those guys injured early on, were coming back into the lineup. The Cougars had begun to have some depth and Walden had a sneaking suspicion that his kids were about to surprise themselves. So why not give them a little tweak to the head game with surprising change in colors?

The first half of the game went as expected with the Cougars falling behind the Huskies. However, the noise level in Martin Stadium was as strong as it had been in Husky Stadium. This was something that was having an effect on the opposition. When the Cougars left the field at halftime there was a collective feeling that they could beat the Huskies rather than a feeling of looming defeat at the hands of the number one PAC 10 team.

Coach Walden gathered his kids. "Nobody believes you can win. You guys are the only ones who can believe in yourselves, besides us coaches. You are the first team to wear all crimson since the 1931 Rose Bowl team. Think about it."

The team all got the chills as that registered.

Walden went on. "You are facing the number one rush defense in the nation today. If you want to win, control the line of scrimmage. You've got to blow them off the line. You can do this. And then, run it right down their throats."

The second half of the game went down just as Walden inspired his kids to play. They ran it right down the Husky's throats. The Cougars physically out hit the Huskies.

One of the key plays that stopped Husky momentum was a Willie Roseburrow run. He was a six foot seven inch, two hundred seventy-five pound tight end. He ran a crossing route and caught a pass. The Cougar defenders walled him in. Willie was moving towards the sideline when Rod came at him head on. Willie did not expect that this much smaller guy would go at him head to head, but that's exactly what Rod did—helmet to helmet contact at full speed. On contact Rod grabbed a handful of jersey, and though he went straight over backwards, he stopped Willie. As Rod got up he was looking at Willie through the ear hole of his helmet.

Mike Peterson, a Cougar offensive receiver and good friend of Rod's asked him on the sidelines, "You're crazy man. Why didn't you just take his legs out?"

"I've been butting faces with bulls, been jerked down by them 2,000 pounders, I ain't ducking my head for nobody." What Rod did not mention was the excruciating pain he felt and the contusion he received in that hit. As he moved across the field he felt like he had a 2 x 4 wedged down the back of his pants. Later he would find out that he had a hairline fracture of his vertebrae. He played the last quarter and a half in severe pain.

A few plays further into the fourth quarter Mike Peterson caught his final collegiate touchdown pass, the one that defeated the Huskies. The Cougars would score another three on a field goal and the game ended with a score of 24-20. The Washington State University Cougars took the Rose Bowl away from their cross state rivals in front of the Pullman, Washington hometown crowd, many of whom never believed it could happen. The odds were too stacked against the Cougars.

Dreams do come true. And, as has been said, "you don't have to be smart if you're lucky. But it doesn't hurt to be prepared."

Jim Walden prepared his kids. Rod was one of those kids. He put his heart and soul into every minute and played with a love of the game and an abandon of all other thought. The lung pain he endured at the beginning of the 1981 season had lessened over time but still plagued him throughout those days at WSU.

Rod was quoted in the papers saying, "I thought a lot about Rocky Blier. He came back after his foot was blown up in Viet Nam and played professional football. I learned not to take things for granted. After I was shot, I thought of the many things I wanted to do in my life, things I wanted to accomplish. You never know how much time you have. I think to myself, I could be six feet underground in a pine box instead of on the field playing football. All the credit goes to the man upstairs."

By the end of the season the Washington State University defenders were ranked ninth in the nation in pass defense and the naysayers that began the year attacking the defense for inexperience were now singing their praises.

The week after the game, on Brooke's birthday, Rod received a letter from the president of the university, Glenn Terrell. It read,

"Dear Rod:

That win over the University of Washington was magnificent—I watched it closely from the stands and from the sidelines. You won it with raw emotion in addition to your skill and effective playing. The leadership of the seniors on the squad was most evident, and all of you have my well-deserved respect.

Sincerely yours,
Glenn Terrell, President."

Rod picks off Kevin Lusk's pass intended for Duck's Rourke Lowe.

Photograph courtesy of the Eugene Register Guard.

EPILOGUE

As Rod was in his last year at WSU he received a contract offer from the Hamilton Tiger-Cats, in Hamilton, Ontario, a pro football team in the Canadian Football League. He was thrilled because this was a major first step toward the NFL. He came bursting into the apartment in Bedrock to announce the news to Patti. She was sitting on the coach, the television on in the background, and Brooke was asleep in her playpen.

"Hun. Look, I got a contract from Bud Riley, the head coach of the Hamilton Tiger-Cats. We're gonna be rich. I'm gonna play pro ball."

"Keep it down, Rod. You're gonna wake Brooke."

"Well, what about the news?" he asked with anticipation.

"What do you mean by, we're gonna be rich? How much did they offer you?" She asked this with a cynical tone.

"Thirty-six thousand for the first year. Hell, I know that ain't big money, but it's a darn good start."

"Thirty-six thousand?" She laughed. "We aren't gonna be rich on no thirty-six thousand. And, I ain't going to Canada."

Rod was stunned by her reaction. "But honey, this is a beginning. Heck, the base pay in the NFL is thirty-four thousand."

"I don't care. I'm not going to Canada." She turned her attention back to the television.

Rod walked out of the apartment. He could not believe what just happened. Patti, the woman he married, the girl who was so nurturing after he was shot, had become sullen in the past months. He was trying to understand what had happened. It was as if Patti had suddenly resented Rod being able to play football.

Rod called home to seek advice. The consensus: bring Patti and Brooke back to John Day, go to Canada and play ball. His dad said, "Son, you can send money home to support your family and in time as things develop for you, she'll probably change her mind. Thirty-six thousand is a darn nice start for you."

Rod said his goodbyes to Coaches Walden and Wheeler, who were very excited about his move to the Canadian pros, then he dropped out of school, packed the family up and got them back to John Day. Patti never said she was happy or proud about Rod's pro contract. In Rod's mind she was doing everything she could to make him feel guilty about leaving.

Rod arrived in Hamilton, Ontario right on schedule, checked in with Bud Riley, was introduced to the equipment manager and got all set up. He practiced hard, applying his usual work ethic and dedication. Each evening he would call John Day and check in with Patti. She gave him little encouragement.

After two weeks Rod was feeling brokenhearted being away from Brooke. He went to see Bud Riley, explained the situation and said, "Coach, I can't tell you how much I appreciate the opportunity. Truth is, my heart's not in it no more. I've got to go home to my family."

Bud was a great guy and surely understood.

Rod wanted to make this life work back in John Day but realized he needed to work, save money, get himself back to WSU and finish getting his degree. Rod picked up a job at the lumber mill. It gave him enough so he could rent a little house for his family. Each month he stashed away a few dollars to put towards his final year of school.

He and Patti decided to have more children together. Today, he is the very proud father of three daughters. The birth of Jaré on September 19, 1984, and the birth of Jacee on April 29, 1991, were days of pride for him only matched by the birth of Brooke in 1981.

The 1983 football season had begun and Rod wanted to see a home game. He gave Coach Walden a call to ask him if he could arrange a sideline pass.

The coach, as always, was glad to hear from him. "Son, come on up and there'll be a pass waiting for you."

"Thanks coach. That'll be great."

"So what are you doing with yourself?" Jim asked.

Rod explained what had happened with his pro career attempt. Jim certainly understood the domestic pressures.

Then he inquired, "What are you doing with yourself now?"

"I'm working in a saw mill, trying to save enough to come back and get my degree so I can teach."

"How much you got left to complete?" Jim asked.

"A year."

"Quit your job. Get your ass back up here. I'll put you on scholarship."

Just like that, Jim Walden with a heart as big as the river his home state was named after, had given Rod Retherford the key to the beginning of a career. Rod could not thank him enough. And to this day Rod will tell you, "If Coach Walden asked me to walk through fire, I'd do it."

Rod graduated a year later with a Bachelor of Science in Secondary Education. He taught high school, but was soon to come across an opportunity to sell insurance, and the combination of salary and commission offered him more income. Without his degree he never would have qualified as a candidate. One of the job's attributes that appealed to Rod was that it would put him on the road. Rod was far better suited for that kind of work than long days in a classroom. His region included most of the country he had covered during his years in rodeo. Yes, he was making less money than he would have as a pro ball player, but he was with his family. Sadly, as happens in a lot of marriages that begin at a young age, Rod and Patti changed and grew apart. Over time their relationship continued to deteriorate into a loveless union.

As he had done with sports, Rod applied himself to his work. Knowing the kind of men who competed in rodeo, and being familiar with all of that lifestyle, he wisely targeted the cowboys to sell his insurance product to. Rod was a friendly and good salesman. The cowboys were takers for the policies. One of those insurance selling trips took Rod to Lewiston, Idaho, along the Snake River. This was territory covered long ago by Lewis and Clark on their famous mapping expedition in search of the inland waterway that would connect the Pacific Ocean to the Mississippi River.

When Rod arrived at the fairgrounds in Lewiston, he saw Larry Grindstaff, an old friend from his younger days when he was a rodeo competitor. The two got to chewing the fat, reminiscing about old times, and catching up on the past twelve years. Larry did a fair amount of teasing about Rod's tie, white shirt, and slacks. Larry had never seen Rod in anything but Wranglers, boots, and a cowboy hat.

While Rod went off to do some insurance selling to a group of cowboys, Larry got word that one of his buddies had turned out of the bull-riding event, and so Larry decided to put Rod's name in as the replacement rider.

Rod got the news from Larry.

"Hell, Larry, I ain't rode in years. And I'm wearing my city clothes."

Larry had an answer. "Don't you worry. We'll scrounge up the gear you'll need."

And he did. They borrowed a little something from any number of cowboys until Rod was outfitted and ready to ride. Aside from Larry, not one of these cowboys knew that Rod was experienced. All they saw was a guy dressed in city duds that they assumed was going to get thrown coming out the gate.

Rod and Larry began playing the idea of his having no experience. It became funnier by the moment as Rod began with questions, "Hey Larry, now what am I supposed to do? I hang onto the rope up here?"

As Rod lowered himself into the chute to mount the bull Larry talked him all the way through it. In the background they had begun hearing the cowboys making bets on whether he would make one second, two, maybe three.

As Rod was about set on the bull Larry added, "Now Rod, don't touch him with your spurs."

Rod was ready for the ride. If he didn't start then he knew he would bust out laughing at all the betting going on in the background. He nodded his head, the gate opened, and two thousand pounds of snorting bull blew out of the chute. With each second that passed the cowboys who were betting on him could not believe his balance and form. This guy, wearing his shirt and tie, his legs covered by borrowed chaps, was almost to eight seconds when he got bucked off.

Rod hit the ground on his feet, turned and headed back to the bucking chute grinning from ear to ear. As he got climbed over the rail he said, "Damn, Larry. I forgot how much fun that is."

The first cowboy said, "You're an asshole." It was not said in anger, but was in exasperation for being had by the joke.

Another said, "Why hell, boy, we done thought you'd never rode before."

Rod interjected. "Tell you what. It's been about twelve years since I rode."

And another said, "You sure made a hell of a ride for not having done it in twelve years."

As Rod and Patti's marriage grew colder, it became a relief for Rod to be on the road selling insurance. He had always enjoyed his time around cowboys and the rodeo. Patti liked watching her brother Scott ride but she had little interest in Rod restarting his rodeo career. When he suggested that he might like to compete again she had little to say.

Rod was at his wits end and sought out the guidance of his dad one afternoon up on the mountain. He had gone up there with his dad to help him do a field clearing. Rod broke down in tears as he described how hollow he felt living in a loveless marriage.

Jim had little comfort to offer his son. As far as he was concerned, the children and the family responsibilities came ahead of anything else. In so many words Jim said, "You made your bed son, now lay in it."

Rod continued to try and find a way towards happiness, but that eventual day from which there would be no turning back arrived. Rod had come to realize that he was useless to his girls if he was living in a depressed state. Perhaps Patti would be a happier person if she was free of Rod. Rod certainly was convinced that their marriage was over.

In 1999 Rod moved out, Patti filed for divorce, and that brought this chapter of his life to a close. Once free of the daily ugliness that the marriage had become, Rod was able to see his daughters under much happier circumstances, although the divorce took a toll on the girls and this continued to haunt him. He rented a room from his old buddy Dennis Adkins and his wife Sherry and began putting a new life together.

Later Rod would run into Stacey Snow at a local Walmart Store. Stacey was the pretty young girl he met twenty years earlier at the September 1976 *Pendleton Round Up*. At this moment he saw Stacey as a grown woman for the first time. She had been married and was raising three sons. Indeed, twenty years earlier they had both been struck by Cupid's arrow. They began dating and are now married. Rod accepted the responsibility of being a step dad to Stacey's sons, Jerin, now twenty-one, Jordan, now nineteen, and Austin, now sixteen, and treated them as if they were his own.

Along Rod's path through life he discovered that he had the patience and skill to be a saddle maker. He builds custom saddles of exceptional quality. He had the privilege of studying with one of the Pacific Northwest's finest saddle makers, Richard Boyer. As Richard took Rod through the exact steps involved in saddle making, the apprentice developed his own book on saddle making, complete with sketches. But the artistic side of it was something that Rod had a natural affinity for. Learning the exact moisture for the leather before the tooling begins, what weight mallet to use, and of course applying his depth of knowledge in horsemanship made Rod very capable of producing a fine saddle.

After the 1982 Apple Cup win, the final game of Rod's college career, a high school teacher and coach by the name of Bill Sieler from Gold Beach, Oregon, a small town in the Pacific Northwest, had sent Rod a tube in the mail. When Rod opened it he found newspaper clippings, notations from the coach, and a note explaining that he, Bill, had followed Rod's football career and had used all those stories in the press to help inspire his young kids, to teach them that they can reach for their dreams. Bill brought tears to Rod's eyes when Bill's note expressed how much it had meant to the little guys to know that a long time ago a little guy just like them was being told he couldn't do it because he was too short.

They would meet twenty-eight years later and Rod would learn that Bill had been a five foot eight inch tall starting quarterback for the University of Washington Huskies in the 1964 Rose Bowl. Bill fully understood what Rod had faced in his high school days and beyond. And Bill completely agreed with Rod when he said, "No matter how big or small you are, its whether you believe in yourself that matters."

Today Rod is an inspirational speaker. One of his recent speaking engagements was at Portland State University following the release of Jeff McQuarie's documentary, *Legends of the Palouse*, www.legendsofthepalouse.com. The film includes an eleven-minute feature on Rod's story. Rod's continuing desire is to encourage the kids, especially the ones who face similar issues as those he managed to overcome.

Rod has said many times, "When you're small—too short, you're a joke to the big guys—until you're not a joke."

For speaking engagements contact:

Seven Locks Press

sevenlocks@aol.com or 714.545.2526

Rod Retherford

rod@rodspeaks.com

www.rodspeaks.com

Rod : 541-279-9060